PRACTICAL PARTY WALLS

Matthew Hearsum
L.LB M.Sc. F.C.I. Arb M.I.E.T.

Solicitor of the Senior Courts of England & Wales
Accredited Mediator

First Printing: 2014

ISBN: 978-1-326-04569-2

Matthew Hearsum
Cleary Court, 169 Church Street East
Woking, Surrey, GU21 6HJ

www.partywallsolicitor.com

Whilst every care has been taken in preparing this publication the statements made are purely for general guidance and cannot be regarded as a substitute for professional advice. No liability is accepted for any loss or expense incurred as the result of relying on statements made in the book.

To my father, John. Thank You.

CONTENTS

Part I – Annotated Party Wall etc. Act 1996

Part II – Case Summaries

Part III - Precedents

Part IV – Historic Acts

ACKNOWLEDGMENTS

I would like thank:

My father, a party wall surveyor, whose words "*you lawyers don't know anything about party walls*" prompted me, as with most children, to prove their parents wrong;

My wife Ellie for her support and patience whilst I was writing this book; and

My paralegal Jennifer for proofreading my drafts.

FOREWORD

Now that the Party Wall etc Act 1996 is of general application throughout the country, there is still a remarkable shortage of useful textbooks or other aids to practitioners or indeed the general public about this legislation which affects so many people.

Matthew Hearsum has produced this short book which, apart from setting out the Act in question, more importantly, cross refers it to the relatively few cases on the subject. There are helpful annotations to the Act itself as well as summaries of the cases themselves. These cases provide a direct insight into the meaning of the various sections of the Act and their application.

I commend this book not only to the party wall practitioners, both surveyors, solicitors and barristers, but also to others such as local authorities and ordinary members of the public who will come across party wall issues whenever they wish to embark on works on or close to their party walls.

Sir Robert Akenhead

High Court Judge of the Technology and Construction Court
Rolls Building, Royal Courts of Justice, London

PREFACE

There are many books available which provide commentary and opinion on the Party Wall etc. Act 1996 and how it should be administered. This is not one of them.

The purpose of this book is not to add to the wealth of opinion already expressed on the 1996 Act, but to provide a quick and easy-to-use reference for party wall surveyors and other professionals allowing them to access the relevant case law, useful precedents and other materials.

If readers think I have missed a relevant case, or that there is a precedent they would find helpful, they are invited to let me know and I will include them in the next edition.

The law is stated as at 1 September 2014

INTRODUCTION

It is testament to the common sense and pragmatism of the surveyors' profession that in the 18 years since the Party Wall Act became law only a handful of cases have reached the Court of Appeal.

As a result there is a marked absence of direct authority on how the provisions of the 1996 Act are to be interpreted. We may therefore look to decisions made in respect of earlier statutes, the London Building Acts. Although these decisions are not binding authority they are a useful example of judicial thinking on the issues.

This book is divided into four parts.

In Part I of this book you will find the provisions of the Party Wall Act annotated with footnotes setting out the relevant case law in which that provision (or an earlier similar provision) has been interpreted.

Part II comprises summaries of the facts and decisions in the cases referred to in Part I.

Part III contains precedents which will hopefully be useful when operating the Act.

Part IV contains extracts from the historic London Building Acts that will assist in interpreting the cases on the 1996 Act.

I hope you find these resources useful.

PART I

THE ANNOTATED PARTY WALL ETC ACT 1996

Section 1

New Building on Line of Junction

(1) This section shall have effect where lands of different owners adjoin and –

(a) are not built on at the line of junction; or

(b) are built on at the line of junction only to the extent of a boundary wall (not being a party fence wall or the external wall of a building),

and either owner is about to build on any part of the line of junction.

(2) If a building owner[1] desires to build a party wall or party fence wall on the line of junction he shall, at least one month before he intends the building work to start, serve on any adjoining owner[2] a notice[3] which indicates his desire to build and describes the intended wall.

---

[1] *See the definition of "building owner" in section 20. The notice must be served by all of the joint owners of the building owner's interest in the land (Lehmann v Herman).*

[2] *See the definition of "adjoining owner" in section 20. The notice must be served on the owners of each separate leasehold and freehold interest (Crosby v Alhambra Company Limited), even if they only occupy a handful of rooms in the building (Fillingham v Wood). It may be possible to serve notice on only one of two or more joint adjoining owners, but the modern law is unclear (Crosby v Alhambra Company Limited). The notice cannot be served on an appointed surveyor without prior express authorisation (Gyle-Thompson v Wall Street Properties).*

[3] *The notice must be sufficiently clear for the adjoining owner to understand what is proposed (Hobbs v Hart & Grover). The notice cannot be served on an appointed surveyor without prior express authorisation (Gyle-Thompson v Wall Street Properties). A failure to date the notice may render it invalid (Bennett v Howell). See precedent 1A.*

Section 1(3)

(3) If, having been served with notice described in subsection (2), an adjoining owner serves on the building owner a notice indicating his consent to the building of a party wall or party fence wall –

(a) the wall shall be built half on the land of each of the two owners or in such other position as may be agreed between the two owners; and

(b) the expense of building the wall shall be from time to time defrayed by the two owners in such proportion as has regard to the use made or to be made of the wall by each of them and to the cost of labour and materials prevailing at the time when that use is made by each owner respectively.

(4) If, having been served with notice described in subsection (2), an adjoining owner does not consent under this subsection to the building of a party wall or party fence wall, the building owner may only build the wall—

(a) at his own expense; and

(b) as an external wall or a fence wall, as the case may be, placed wholly on his own land,

and consent under this subsection is consent by a notice served within the period of fourteen days beginning with the day on which the notice described in subsection (2) is served.

(5) If the building owner[4] desires to build on the line of junction a wall placed wholly on his own land he shall, at least one month before he intends the building work to start, serve on any adjoining owner[5] a notice[6] which indicates his desire to build and describes the intended wall.

(6) Where the building owner builds a wall wholly on his own land in accordance with subsection (4) or (5) he shall have the right, at any time in the period which—

(a) begins one month after the day on which the notice mentioned in the subsection concerned was served, and

(b) ends twelve months after that day,

to place below the level of the land of the adjoining owner such projecting footings and foundations as are necessary for the construction of the wall.

---

[4] *See the definition of "building owner" in section 20. The notice must be served by all of the joint owners of the building owner's interest in the land (Lehmann v Herman).*

[5] *See the definition of "adjoining owner" in section 20. The notice must be served on the owners of each separate leasehold and freehold interest (Crosby v Alhambra Company Limited), even if they only occupy a handful of rooms in the building (Fillingham v Wood). It may be possible to serve notice on only one of two or more joint adjoining owners, but the modern law is unclear (Crosby v Alhambra Company Limited). The notice cannot be served on an appointed surveyor without prior express authorisation (Gyle-Thompson v Wall Street Properties).*

[6] *The notice must be sufficiently clear for the adjoining owner to understand what is proposed (Hobbs v Hart & Grover). The notice cannot be served on an appointed surveyor without prior express authorisation (Gyle-Thompson v Wall Street Properties). A failure to date the notice may render it invalid (Bennett v Howell). See precedent 1B.*

Section 1(7)

(7) Where the building owner builds a wall wholly on his own land in accordance with subsection (4) or (5) he shall do so at his own expense and shall compensate any adjoining owner and any adjoining occupier for any damage to his property occasioned by—

(a) the building of the wall;

(b) the placing of any footings or foundations placed in accordance with subsection (6).

(8) Where any dispute[7] arises under this section between the building owner and any adjoining owner or occupier it is to be determined in accordance with section 10.

---

[7] *There is no "deemed dispute" provision as with sections 5 and 6. Only actual disputes may be referred to the tribunal of surveyors.*

Section 2

Repair etc of a Party Wall: Rights of Owner

(1) This section applies where lands of different owners adjoin and at the line of junction the said lands are built on or a boundary wall, being a party fence wall or the external wall of a building, has been erected.

(2) A building owner shall have the following rights—

(a) to underpin, thicken or raise[8] a party structure, a party fence wall, or an external wall which belongs to the building owner and is built against a party structure or party fence wall;

(b) to make good, repair, or demolish and rebuild[9], a party structure or party fence wall in a case where such work is necessary on account of defect or want of repair[10] of the structure or wall;

---

[8] *This does not include the right to lower the height of a party wall (Gyle-Thompson v Wall Street Properties), but see subsection (e) below. Nor does it include the right to "raise a party wall downwards" – this is underpinning (Standard Bank of British South America v Stokes).*

[9] *The building owner must rebuild a party wall to substantially the same design, and may not rebuild it to a different design, for example by including an arch that was not there previously (Burlington Property Company Limited v Odeon Theatres Limited) or to a lesser height than before (Gyle-Thompson v Wall Street Properties); but see subsection (e). There is no right to rebuild a party wall partly on the adjoining owners land unless notice has been served (Rashid v Sharif).*

[10] *If the damage was caused by a third party (e.g. a tenant) only half the cost of repair can be recovered against that third party (Apostal v Simons) because the owner only owns half of the wall. The balance is, presumably, recoverable by owner of the other half. Dampness does not of itself constitute disrepair unless is makes the wall less effective for the purposes for which it is used or intended to be used (Barry v Minturn).*

Section 2(2)(c)

(c) to demolish a partition which separates buildings belonging to different owners but does not conform with statutory requirements and to build instead a party wall which does so conform;

(d) in the case of buildings connected by arches or structures over public ways or over passages belonging to other persons, to demolish the whole or part of such buildings, arches or structures which do not conform with statutory requirements and to rebuild them so that they do so conform;

(e) to demolish a party structure which is of insufficient strength or height for the purposes of any intended building of the building owner and to rebuild it of sufficient strength or height for the said purposes (including rebuilding to a lesser height or thickness where the rebuilt structure is of sufficient strength and height for the purposes of any adjoining owner);

(f) to cut into a party structure[11] for any purpose (which may be or include the purpose of inserting a damp proof course);

(g) to cut away from a party wall, party fence wall, external wall or boundary wall any footing or any projecting chimney breast, jamb or flue, or other projection on or over the land of the building owner in order to erect, raise or underpin any such wall or for any other purpose;

---

[11] *This includes removing plaster with percussive tools, but not manual tools (Kelliher v Ash Estates Limited).*

(h) to cut away or demolish parts of any wall or building of an adjoining owner overhanging the land of the building owner or overhanging a party wall, to the extent that it is necessary to cut away or demolish the parts to enable a vertical wall to be erected or raised against the wall or building of the adjoining owner;

(j) to cut into the wall of an adjoining owner's building in order to insert a flashing or other weather-proofing of a wall erected against that wall;

(k) to execute any other necessary works incidental to the connection of a party structure with the premises adjoining it;

(l) to raise a party fence wall, or to raise such a wall for use as a party wall, and to demolish a party fence wall and rebuild it as a party fence wall or as a party wall[12];

(m) subject to the provisions of section 11(7), to reduce, or to demolish and rebuild, a party wall or party fence wall to—

   (i) a height of not less than two metres where the wall is not used by an adjoining owner to any greater extent than a boundary wall; or

   (ii) a height currently enclosed upon by the building of an adjoining owner;

---

[12] *The building owner must rebuild a party wall to substantially the same design, and may not rebuild it to a different design by e.g. incorporating an archway where there was none before (Burlington Property Company Limited v Odeon Theatres Limited) or to a lesser height than before (Gyle-Thompson v Wall Street Properties);but see subsection (e).*

Section 2(2)(n)

(n) to expose a party wall or party structure hitherto enclosed subject to providing adequate weathering[13].

(3) Where work mentioned in paragraph (a) of subsection (2) is not necessary on account of defect or want of repair of the structure or wall concerned, the right falling within that paragraph is exercisable—

(a) subject to making good[14] all damage occasioned by the work to the adjoining premises or to their internal furnishings and decorations; and

(b) where the work is to a party structure or external wall, subject to carrying any relevant flues and chimney stacks up to such a height and in such materials as may be agreed between the building owner and the adjoining owner concerned or, in the event of dispute, determined in accordance with section 10;

and relevant flues and chimney stacks are those which belong to an adjoining owner and either form part of or rest on or against the party structure or external wall.

(4) The right falling within subsection (2)(e) is exercisable subject to—

(a) making good[14] all damage occasioned by the work to the adjoining premises or to their internal furnishings and decorations; and

---

[13] *This may be an ongoing and indefinite obligation to provide adequate weathering (Marchant v Capital and County Plc).*

[14] *The adjoining owner is not bound to allow the building owner's contractors to make good; under section 11(8) they can elect to require the building owner to pay a sum of money in lieu of making good.*

(b) carrying any relevant flues and chimney stacks up to such a height and in such materials as may be agreed between the building owner and the adjoining owner concerned or, in the event of dispute, determined in accordance with section 10;

and relevant flues and chimney stacks are those which belong to an adjoining owner and either form part of or rest on or against the party structure.

(5) Any right falling within subsection (2)(f), (g) or (h) is exercisable subject to making good[14] all damage occasioned by the work to the adjoining premises or to their internal furnishings and decorations.

(6) The right falling within subsection (2)(j) is exercisable subject to making good[14] all damage occasioned by the work to the wall of the adjoining owner's building.

(7) The right falling within subsection (2)(m) is exercisable subject to—

(a) reconstructing any parapet or replacing an existing parapet with another one; or

(b) constructing a parapet where one is needed but did not exist before.

(8) For the purposes of this section a building or structure which was erected before the day on which this Act was passed shall be deemed to conform with statutory requirements if it conforms with the statutes regulating buildings or structures on the date on which it was erected.

Section 3
Party Structure Notices

(1) Before exercising any right conferred on him by section 2 a building owner[15] shall serve[16] on any adjoining owner[17] a notice[18] (in this Act referred to as a "party structure notice") stating—

(a) the name and address of the building owner;

(b) the nature and particulars of the proposed work[19] including, in cases where the building owner proposes to construct special foundations, plans, sections and details of construction of the special foundations together with reasonable particulars of the loads to be carried thereby; and

---

[15] *See the definition of "building owner" in section 20. The notice must be served by all of the joint owners of the building owner's interest in the land (Lehmann v Herman).*

[16] *See the service provisions in section 15. The notice cannot be served on an appointed surveyor without prior express authorisation (Gyle-Thompson v Wall Street Properties).*

[17] *See the definition of "adjoining owner" in section 20. The notice must be served on the owners of each separate leasehold and freehold interest (Crosby v Alhambra Company Limited), even if they only occupy a handful of rooms in the building (Fillingham v Wood). It may be possible to serve notice on only one of two or more joint adjoining owners, but the modern law is unclear (Crosby v Alhambra Company Limited).*

[18] *See Precedent 3A.*

[19] *The notice must be sufficiently clear for the adjoining owner to understand what is proposed (Hobbs v Hart & Grover).*

(c) the date[20] on which the proposed work will begin.

(2) A party structure notice shall—

(a) be served at least two months before the date on which the proposed work will begin;

(b) cease to have effect if the work to which it relates—

(i) has not begun within the period of twelve months[21] beginning with the day on which the notice is served; and

(ii) is not prosecuted with due diligence.

(3) Nothing in this section shall—

(a) Prevent a building owner from exercising with the consent in writing[22] of the adjoining owners and of the adjoining occupiers any right conferred on him by section 2; or

(b) require a building owner to serve any party structure notice before complying with any notice served under any statutory provisions relating to dangerous or neglected structures.

---

[20] *A failure to date the notice may render it invalid (Bennett v Howell).*

[21] *It has been held that this period only applies where the adjoining owner consents to a notice, and not where a dispute has arisen and been determined by award (Leadbetter v Marylebone Corporation [No. 2]).*

[22] *It is not necessary to serve a party structure notice if there is a written agreement with all parties authorising the works (Bennett v Harrod's Stores Limited) however an oral agreement over the garden fence is insufficient (Seeff v Ho).*

Section 4
Counter Notices

(1) An adjoining owner may, having been served with a party structure notice serve on the building owner a notice (in this Act referred to as a "counter notice") setting out—

(a) in respect of a party fence wall or party structure, a requirement that the building owner build in or on the wall or structure to which the notice relates such chimney copings, breasts, jambs or flues, or such piers or recesses or other like works, as may reasonably be required for the convenience of the adjoining owner[23];

(b) in respect of special foundations to which the adjoining owner consents under section 7(4) below, a requirement that the special foundations—

(i) be placed at a specified greater depth than that proposed by the building owner; or

(ii) be constructed of sufficient strength to bear the load to be carried by columns of any intended building of the adjoining owner,

or both.[24]

(2) A counter notice shall—

(a) specify the works required by the notice to be executed and shall be accompanied by plans, sections and particulars of such works; and

(b) be served within the period of one month beginning with the day on which the party structure notice is served.

---

[23] *See Precedent 4A*
[24] *See Precedent 4B*

(3) A building owner on whom a counter notice has been served shall comply with the requirements of the counter notice unless the execution of the works required by the counter notice would—

(a) be injurious to him;

(b) cause unnecessary inconvenience to him; or

(c) cause unnecessary delay in the execution of the works pursuant to the party structure notice.

Section 5

Disputes under sections 3 and 4

If an owner on whom a party structure notice or a counter notice has been served does not serve a notice indicating his consent to it within the period of fourteen days beginning with the day on which the party structure notice or counter notice was served, he shall be deemed to have dissented from the notice and a dispute shall be deemed to have arisen between the parties.

Section 6

Adjacent Excavation and Construction

(1) This section applies where—

(a) a building owner proposes to excavate, or excavate for and erect a building or structure, within a distance of three metres measured horizontally from any part of a building or structure of an adjoining owner; and

(b) any part of the proposed excavation, building or structure will within those three metres extend to a lower level than the level of the bottom of the foundations of the building or structure of the adjoining owner.

(2) This section also applies where—

(a) a building owner proposes to excavate, or excavate for and erect a building or structure, within a distance of six metres measured horizontally from any part of a building or structure of an adjoining owner; and

(b) any part of the proposed excavation, building or structure will within those six metres meet a plane drawn downwards in the direction of the excavation, building or structure of the building owner at an angle of forty-five degrees to the horizontal from the line formed by the intersection of the plane of the level of the bottom of the foundations of the building or structure of the adjoining owner with the plane of the external face of the external wall of the building or structure of the adjoining owner.

(3) The building owner may, and if required by the adjoining owner shall, at his own expense underpin or otherwise strengthen or safeguard the foundations of the building or structure of the adjoining owner so far as may be necessary.

Section 6(4)

(4) Where the buildings or structures of different owners are within the respective distances mentioned in subsections (1) and (2) the owners of those buildings or structures shall be deemed to be adjoining owners for the purposes of this section.

(5) In any case where this section applies the building owner[25] shall, at least one month[26] before beginning to excavate, or excavate for and erect a building or structure, serve on the adjoining owner[27] a notice indicating his proposals[28] and stating whether he proposes to underpin or otherwise strengthen or safeguard the foundations of the building or structure of the adjoining owner.

---

[25] *See the definition of "building owner" in section 20. The notice must be served by all of the joint owners of the building owner's interest in the land (Lehmann v Herman).*

[26] *A failure to date the notice may render it invalid (Bennett v Howell).*

[27] *See the definition of "adjoining owner" in section 20. The notice must be served on the owners of each separate leasehold and freehold interest (Crosby v Alhambra Company Limited), even if they only occupy a handful of rooms in the building (Fillingham v Wood). It may be possible to serve notice on only one of two or more joint owners, but the modern law is unclear (Crosby v Alhambra Company Limited). The notice (and any award) cannot be served on an appointed surveyor without prior express authorisation (Gyle-Thompson v Wall Street Properties).*

[28] *The notice must be sufficiently clear for the adjoining owner to understand what is proposed (Hobbs v Hart & Grover).*

(6) The notice referred to in subsection (5) shall be accompanied[29] by plans and sections showing—

(a) the site and depth of any excavation the building owner proposes to make;

(b) if he proposes to erect a building or structure, its site.

(7) If an owner on whom a notice referred to in subsection (5) has been served does not serve a notice indicating his consent to it within the period of fourteen days beginning with the day on which the notice referred to in subsection (5) was served, he shall be deemed to have dissented from the notice and a dispute shall be deemed to have arisen between the parties.

(8) The notice referred to in subsection (5) shall cease to have effect if the work to which the notice relates—

(a) has not begun within the period of twelve months beginning with the day on which the notice was served; and

(b) is not prosecuted with due diligence.

(9) On completion of any work executed in pursuance of this section the building owner shall if so requested by the adjoining owner supply him with particulars including plans and sections of the work.

(10) Nothing in this section shall relieve the building owner from any liability to which he would otherwise be subject for injury to any adjoining owner or any adjoining occupier by reason of work executed by him.

---

[29] *A notice that does not comply with these requirements will not be valid (Hobbs, Hart & Co v Grover).*

Section 7

Compensation etc.

(1) A building owner[30] shall not exercise any right conferred on him by this Act in such a manner or at such time as to cause unnecessary inconvenience[31] to any adjoining owner or to any adjoining occupier.

(2) The building owner shall compensate any adjoining owner and any adjoining occupier for any loss or damage[32] which may result to any of them by reason of any work executed in pursuance of this Act.

---

[30] *This duty is personal to the building owner, and cannot be delegated to their contractors (Jolliffe v Woodhouse). It is unlikely that this liability will transfer to a subsequent purchaser, but instead remains with the building owner.*

[31] *Adjoining owners are expected to tolerate a certain degree of discomfort. It is only where the building owner fails to take a reasonable step to abate any inconvenience that he will become liable (Andrae v Selfridge & Co). A delay of 12 weeks was held to be unreasonable (Kelliher v Ash Estates Limited). If the works can be done in an equally effective way at no or modest extra cost, but with less inconvenience to the adjoining owner, then the surveyors ought to award those alternative works (Barry v Minturn)*

Where works take longer than is reasonably necessary the building owner may be liable for causing unnecessary inconvenience (Jolliffe v Woodhouse). It has been held that a 12 week delay in the works comprised unreasonable inconvenience (Kelliher v Ash Estates Limited).

[32] *This may include damages for loss of trade (Adams v Marylebone Borough Council), loss of earnings or loss of amenity (Kelliher v Ash Estates Limited). Only half the cost of repair can be recovered against a third party wrongdoer that caused damage to the wall (Apostal v Simons). Where there is no clear intention to undertake remedial works a claim may be limited to diminution in value (Bruer v Leccacorvi).*

(3) Where a building owner in exercising any right conferred on him by this Act lays open any part of the adjoining land or building he shall at his own expense make and maintain so long as may be necessary a proper hoarding, shoring or fans or temporary construction for the protection of the adjoining land or building and the security of any adjoining occupier.

(4) Nothing in this Act shall authorise the building owner to place special foundations on land of an adjoining owner without his previous consent in writing[33].

(5) Any works executed in pursuance of this Act shall—

(a) comply with the provisions of statutory requirements; and

(b) be executed in accordance with such plans, sections and particulars as may be agreed between the owners or in the event of dispute determined in accordance with section 10;

and no deviation shall be made from those plans, sections and particulars except such as may be agreed between the owners (or surveyors acting on their behalf) or in the event of dispute determined in accordance with section 10.

---

[33] *A common solution is for consent is granted in exchange for waiver of a contribution by the adjoining owner under section 11. See Precedent 7A.*

Section 8
Rights of Entry

(1) A building owner, his servants, agents and workmen may during usual working hours enter and remain on any land or premises for the purpose of executing any work in pursuance of this Act and may remove any furniture or fittings or take any other action necessary for that purpose.

(2) If the premises are closed, the building owner, his agents and workmen may, if accompanied by a constable or other police officer, break open any fences or doors in order to enter the premises.

(3) No land or premises may be entered by any person under subsection (1) unless the building owner serves on the owner and the occupier of the land or premises—

(a) in case of emergency, such notice of the intention to enter as may be reasonably practicable;

(b) in any other case, such notice of the intention to enter as complies with subsection (4).

(4) Notice complies with this subsection if it is served in a period of not less than fourteen days ending with the day of the proposed entry[34].

(5) A surveyor appointed or selected under section 10 may during usual working hours enter and remain on any land or premises for the purpose of carrying out the object for which he is appointed or selected.

(6) No land or premises may be entered by a surveyor under subsection (5) unless the building owner who is a party to the dispute concerned serves on the owner and the occupier of the land or premises—

---

[34] *See Precedent 8A.*

(a) in case of emergency, such notice of the intention to enter as may be reasonably practicable;

(b) in any other case, such notice of the intention to enter as complies with subsection.

Section 9
Easements

Nothing in this Act shall—

(a) authorise any interference[35] with an easement of light or other easements in or relating to a party wall; or

(b) prejudicially affect any right of any person to preserve or restore any right or other thing in or connected with a party wall in case of the party wall being pulled down or rebuilt

---

[35] *The surveyors may authorise a temporary interference with an easement during the works, but may not authorise a permanent interference (Crofts v Haldane).*

Section 10
Resolution of Disputes

(1) Where a dispute arises or is deemed to have arisen between a building owner and an adjoining owner in respect of any matter connected with any work to which this Act relates either—

(a) both parties shall concur in the appointment of one surveyor (in this section referred to as an "agreed surveyor"); or

(b) each party shall appoint a surveyor and the two surveyors so appointed shall forthwith select a third surveyor (all of whom are in this section referred to as "the three surveyors").

(2) All appointments and selections made under this section shall be in writing[36] and shall not be rescinded by either party.

(3) If an agreed surveyor—

(a) refuses to act;

(b) neglects to act for a period of ten days beginning with the day on which either party serves a request[37] on him;

(c) dies before the dispute is settled; or

(d) becomes or deems himself incapable of acting,

the proceedings for settling such dispute shall begin *de novo.*

---

[36] *An award made by surveyors that have not been appointed in writing is invalid (Gyle-Thompson v Wall Street Properties). It was suggested by the Court that surveyors ought to ask to see each other's letter of appointment.*

[37] *See Precedent 10A.*

Section 10(4)

(4) If either party to the dispute—

(a) refuses to appoint a surveyor under subsection (1)(b), or

(b) neglects to appoint a surveyor under subsection (1)(b) for a period of ten days beginning with the day on which the other party serves a request[38] on him,

the other party may make the appointment on his behalf.

(5) If, before the dispute is settled, a surveyor appointed under paragraph (b) of subsection (1) by a party to the dispute dies, or becomes or deems himself incapable of acting, the party who appointed him may appoint another surveyor in his place with the same power and authority.

(6) If a surveyor—

(a) appointed under paragraph (b) of subsection (1) by a party to the dispute; or

(b) appointed under subsection (4) or (5),

refuses to act effectively, the surveyor of the other party may proceed to act ex parte and anything so done by him shall be as effectual as if he had been an agreed surveyor.

---

[38] *See Precedent 10B.*

(7) If a surveyor—

(a) appointed under paragraph (b) of subsection (1) by a party to the dispute; or

(b) appointed under subsection (4) or (5),

neglects to act effectively[39] for a period of ten days[40] beginning with the day on which either party or the surveyor of the other party serves a request[41] on him, the surveyor of the other party may proceed to act ex parte in respect of the subject matter of the request and anything so done by him shall be as effectual as if he had been an agreed surveyor

(8) If either surveyor appointed under subsection (1)(b) by a party to the dispute refuses to select a third surveyor under subsection (1) or (9), or neglects to do so for a period of ten days beginning with the day on which the other surveyor serves a request[42] on him—

(a) the appointing officer; or

(b) in cases where the relevant appointing officer or his employer is a party to the dispute, the Secretary of State,

---

[39] *To act effectively a surveyor must address the subject matter of the request and set out their position. That the other surveyor does not agree with them does not mean that they have failed to act effectively (Patel v Peters).*

[40] *An effective reply received outside the 10 day period will bring to an end the power to make an award ex parte (Patel v Peters).*

[41] *See Precedent 10C.*

[42] *See Precedent 10D.*

may on the application of either surveyor select a third surveyor who shall have the same power and authority as if he had been selected under subsection (1) or subsection (9).

(9) If a third surveyor selected under subsection (1)(b)—

(a) refuses to act;

(b) neglects to act for a period of ten days beginning with the day on which either party or the surveyor appointed by either party serves a request[43] on him; or

(c) dies, or becomes or deems himself incapable of acting, before the dispute is settled,

the other two of the three surveyors shall forthwith select another surveyor in his place with the same power and authority.

(10) The agreed surveyor or as the case may be the three surveyors or any two of them shall settle by award[44] any matter—

(a) which is connected with any work to which this Act relates, and

(b) which is in dispute between the building owner and the adjoining owner.

---

[43] *See Precedent 10E.*

[44] *Awards made by the tribunal of surveyors are not arbitration awards (Chartered Society of Physiotherapy v Simmonds Church Smiles). The determination is in a class of its own, more akin to an expert determination than arbitration (Zissis v Lukomski). Awards are not capable of registration at HM Land Registry (Observatory Hill Limited v Camtel Investments SA).*

(11) Either of the parties or either of the surveyors appointed by the parties may call upon the third surveyor selected in pursuance of this section to determine the disputed matters and he shall make the necessary award.

(12) An award may determine[45]—

(a) the right to execute any work[46];

(b) the time and manner of executing any work; and

(c) any other matter[47] arising out of or incidental to the dispute including the costs of making the award;

but any period appointed by the award for executing any work shall not unless otherwise agreed between the building owner and the adjoining owner begin to run until after the expiration of the period prescribed by this Act for service of the notice in respect of which the dispute arises or is deemed to have arisen.

---

[45] *The surveyors can determine issues of law, however they must be issues within their jurisdiction, and their determination is not final, and is subject to review on appeal (Loost v Kremer).*

[46] *The surveyors can only deal with issues that arise out of the works for which they are appointed, and cannot deal with potential future works (Leadbetter v Marylebone Corporation [No. 1]).*

[47] *The surveyors may authorise a temporary interference with the adjoining owner's property rights during the works, but has no jurisdiction to authorise permanent interference (Crofts v Haldene; see also section 9).*

Section 10(13)

(13) The reasonable costs[48] incurred in—

(a) making or obtaining an award under this section;

(b) reasonable inspections of work to which the award relates; and

(d) any other matter arising out of the dispute,

shall be paid by such of the parties[49] as the surveyor or surveyors making the award determine.

(14) Where the surveyors appointed by the parties make an award the surveyors shall serve it forthwith on the parties.

(15) Where an award is made by the third surveyor—

(a) he shall, after payment of the costs of the award, serve it forthwith on the parties or their appointed surveyors; and

(b) if it is served on their appointed surveyors, they shall serve it forthwith on the parties.

(16) The award shall be conclusive and shall not except as provided by this section be questioned in any court.

---

[48] *This does not include the legal costs incurred in preparing for legal proceedings that were subsequently avoided (Reeves v Blake).*

[49] *An award that provides for the fees to be paid to the surveyors, rather than their owners, is probably invalid (Onigbanjo v Pearson).*

(17) Either of the parties to the dispute may, within the period of fourteen days[50] beginning with the day on which an award made under this section is served on him[51], appeal[52] to the county court[53] against the award and the county court may—

(a) rescind the award or modify it in such manner as the court thinks fit; and

(b) make such order as to costs as the court thinks fit.

---

[50] *The 14 day time limit only applies to valid awards. Where an award is invalid, or beyond the surveyors jurisdiction, it may be challenged at any time (Gyle-Thompson v Wall Street Properties).*

[51] *The appeal must be issued within 14 days of the award being deemed served under section 15 (Freetown Limited v Assethold Limited), or within 14 days of actual receipt if sooner. An award is served on a party when it is received by that party, and not when it was received by the other parties (Riley Gowler Ltd v National Heart Hospital).*

[52] *An appeal under s.10(17) is made under Part 52 of the Civil Procedure Rules (Zissis v Lukomski). Appeals under this section have historically been by way of rehearing, meaning that the Court may approach the matter afresh and does not have to find the award was wrong before modifying or rescinding it (Chartered Society of Physiotherapy v Simmonds Church Smiles; Zissis v Lukomski). However the position may have changed following the 2012 update of the Civil Procedure Rules.*

[53] *The appeal must be issued in the County Court only, but may, if appropriate, be transferred to the High Court for hearing (Kaye v Lawrence).*

Section 11

Expenses

(1) Except as provided under this section expenses of work under this Act shall be defrayed by the building owner.

(2) Any dispute as to responsibility for expenses shall be settled as provided in section 10.

(3) An expense mentioned in section 1(3)(b) shall be defrayed as there mentioned.

(4) Where work is carried out in exercise of the right mentioned in section 2(2)(a), and the work is necessary on account of defect or want of repair of the structure or wall concerned, the expenses shall be defrayed by the building owner and the adjoining owner in such proportion as has regard to—

 (a) the use which the owners respectively make or may make of the structure or wall concerned; and

 (b) responsibility for the defect or want of repair concerned, if more than one owner makes use of the structure or wall concerned.

(5) Where work is carried out in exercise of the right mentioned in section 2(2)(b) the expenses shall be defrayed by the building owner and the adjoining owner in such proportion as has regard to—

 (a) the use which the owners respectively make or may make of the structure or wall concerned; and

 (b) responsibility for the defect or want of repair concerned, if more than one owner makes use of the structure or wall concerned.

(6) Where the adjoining premises are laid open in exercise of the right mentioned in section 2(2)(e) a fair allowance in respect of disturbance and inconvenience shall be paid by the building owner to the adjoining owner or occupier.

(7) Where a building owner proposes to reduce the height of a party wall or party fence wall under section 2(2)(m) the adjoining owner may serve a counter notice under section 4 requiring the building owner to maintain the existing height of the wall, and in such case the adjoining owner shall pay to the building owner a due proportion of the cost of the wall so far as it exceeds—

(a) two metres in height; or

(b) the height currently enclosed upon by the building of the adjoining owner.

(8) Where the building owner is required to make good damage under this Act[54] the adjoining owner has a right to require that the expenses of such making good be determined in accordance with section 10 and paid to him in lieu of the carrying out of work to make the damage good.

(9) Where—

(a) works are carried out, and

(b) some of the works are carried out at the request of the adjoining owner or in pursuance of a requirement made by him,

he shall defray the expenses of carrying out the works requested or required by him.

---

[54] *These are the rights conferred by section 2(2)(a), (e), (f), (g), (h) and (j).*

Section 11(10)

(10) Where—

(a) consent in writing has been given to the construction of special foundations on land of an adjoining owner; and

(b) the adjoining owner erects any building or structure and its cost is found to be increased by reason of the existence of the said foundations,

the owner of the building to which the said foundations belong shall, on receiving an account[55] with any necessary invoices and other supporting documents within the period of two months beginning with the day of the completion of the work by the adjoining owner, repay to the adjoining owner so much of the cost as is due to the existence of the said foundations.

(11) Where use is subsequently made by the adjoining owner of work carried out solely at the expense of the building owner the adjoining owner shall pay a due proportion of the expenses incurred by the building owner[56] in carrying out that work; and for this purpose he shall be taken to have incurred expenses calculated by reference to what the cost of the work would be if it were carried out at the time when that subsequent use is made.

---

[55] *See Precedent 11A.*

[56] *The right to receive compensation is transferred to a purchaser on the sale of a freehold (Mason v Fulham Corporation) but the right does not pass from a landlord to a tenant on the grant of a lease (Re: Stone & Hastie).*

Section 12

Security for expenses

(1) An adjoining owner may serve a notice[57] requiring the building owner before he begins any work in the exercise of the rights conferred by this Act[58] to give such security as may be agreed between the owners or in the event of dispute determined in accordance with section 10[59].

(2) Where—

(a) in the exercise of the rights conferred by this Act an adjoining owner requires the building owner to carry out any work the expenses of which are to be defrayed in whole or in part by the adjoining owner; or

(b) an adjoining owner serves a notice on the building owner under subsection (1),

the building owner may before beginning the work to which the requirement or notice relates serve a notice[60] on the adjoining owner requiring him to give such security as may be agreed between the owners or in the event of dispute determined in accordance with section 10.

---

[57] *See Precedent 12A.*

[58] *The adjoining owner may request security in respect of any works under this Act, irrespective of whether they are on the building owner's land or the adjoining owner's land (Kaye v Lawrence).*

[59] *If security is requested the surveyors cannot refuse it, but they can decide the amount to be awarded, even if it is only a nominal sum (Capital & Leisure Hotels v Independant Estates Plc).*

[60] *See Precedent 12B.*

Section 12(3)

(3) If within the period of one month beginning with—

(a) the day on which a notice is served under subsection (2); or

(b) in the event of dispute, the date of the determination by the surveyor or surveyors,

the adjoining owner does not comply with the notice or the determination, the requirement or notice by him to which the building owner's notice under that subsection relates shall cease to have effect.

Section 13
Account for work carried out

(1) Within the period of two months[61] beginning with the day of the completion of any work executed by a building owner of which the expenses are to be wholly or partially defrayed by an adjoining owner in accordance with section 11 the building owner shall serve on the adjoining owner an account in writing[62] showing—

(a) particulars and expenses of the work[63]; and

(b) any deductions to which the adjoining owner or any other person is entitled in respect of old materials or otherwise;

and in preparing the account the work shall be estimated and valued at fair average rates and prices according to the nature of the work, the locality and the cost of labour and materials prevailing at the time when the work is executed.

(2) Within the period of one month beginning with the day of service of the said account the adjoining owner may serve on the building owner a notice stating any objection he may have thereto and thereupon a dispute shall be deemed to have arisen between the parties.

---

[61] *There are conflicting authorities on how strict the two month time limit is. In J. Jarvis & Sons Ltd v Baker it was held that the two month limit was not mandatory, and an account could still be served outside of that period. However the opposite conclusion was reached in Spiers & Sons Ltd v Troup.*

[62] *See Precedent 13A.*

[63] *Minor defects in an account will probably not invalidate it, provided it is possible for the recipient to calculate how much they are required to pay (Reading v Barnard).*

Section 13(3)

(3) If within that period of one month the adjoining owner does not serve notice under subsection (2) he shall be deemed to have no objection to the account.

Section 14
Settlement of Account

(1) All expenses to be defrayed by an adjoining owner in accordance with an account served under section 13 shall be paid by the adjoining owner.

(2) Until an adjoining owner pays to the building owner[64] such expenses as aforesaid the property in any works executed under this Act to which the expenses relate shall be vested solely in the building owner.

---

[64] *These sums are to paid to the owner of the building owner's land when the use is made which may be different to building owner tat undertook the works (Mason v Fulham Corporation).*

Section 15
Services of notices etc.

(1) A notice or other document required or authorised to be served under this Act may be served[65] on a person[66]—

(a) by delivering it to him in person;

(b) by sending it by post[67] to him at his usual or last-known residence or place of business in the United Kingdom; or

(c) in the case of a body corporate, by delivering it to the secretary or clerk of the body corporate at its registered or principal office or sending it by post to the secretary or clerk of that body corporate at that office.

(2) In the case of a notice or other document required or authorised to be served under this Act on a person as owner of premises, it may alternatively be served by—

(a) addressing it "the owner" of the premises (naming them), and

(b) delivering it to a person on the premises or, if no person to whom it can be delivered is found there, fixing it to a conspicuous part of the premises.

---

[65] *An award is served on a party when it is received by that party, and not when it was received by the other parties (Riley Gowler Ltd v National Heart Hospital).*

[66] *An award can only be served on the parties, and not on their surveyors (Gyle-Thompson v Wall Street Properties).*

[67] *The notice or other document is deemed served when it would have been received in the ordinary course of post, unless the recipient can prove that he did not receive it (Freetown Limited v Assethold Limited). This is second business day after posting for first class post, or fourth business day for second class post.*

Section 16
Offences

(1) If—

(a) an occupier of land or premises refuses to permit a person to do anything which he is entitled to do with regard to the land or premises under section 8(1) or (5); and

(b) the occupier knows or has reasonable cause to believe that the person is so entitled,

the occupier is guilty of an offence.

(2) If—

(a) a person hinders or obstructs a person in attempting to do anything which he is entitled to do with regard to land or premises under section 8(1) or (5); and

(b) the first-mentioned person knows or has reasonable cause to believe that the other person is so entitled,

the first-mentioned person is guilty of an offence.

(3) A person guilty of an offence under subsection (1) or (2) is liable on summary conviction to a fine of an amount not exceeding level 3[68] on the standard scale.

---

[68] *£1,000 as at date of publication.*

Section 17

Recovery of sums

Any sum payable in pursuance of this Act (otherwise than by way of fine) shall be recoverable summarily[69] as a civil debt.

---

[69] *This refers to the summary procedure in section 58 of the Magistrates Court Act 1980. See Precedents 17A to E.*

Section 18

Exception in case of Temples

(1) This Act shall not apply to land which is situated in inner London and in which there is an interest belonging to

(a) the Honourable Society of the Inner Temple,

(b) the Honourable Society of the Middle Temple,

(c) the Honourable Society of Lincoln's Inn, or

(d) the Honourable Society of Gray's Inn.

(2) The reference in subsection (1) to inner London is to Greater London other than the outer London boroughs.

Section 19
The Crown

(1) This Act shall apply to land in which there is-

(a) an interest belonging to Her Majesty in right of the Crown,

(b) an interest belonging to a government department, or

(c) an interest held in trust for Her Majesty for the purposes of any such department.

(2) This Act shall apply to—

(a) land which is vested in, but not occupied by, Her Majesty in right of the Duchy of Lancaster;

(b) land which is vested in, but not occupied by, the possessor for the time being of the Duchy of Cornwall.

Section 20
Interpretation

(1) In this Act, unless the context otherwise requires, the following expressions have the meanings hereby respectively assigned to them—

"*adjoining owner*" and "*adjoining occupier*" respectively mean any owner and any occupier of land[70], buildings, storeys or rooms[71] adjoining those of the building owner and for the purposes only of section 6 within the distances specified in that section;

"*appointing officer*" means the person appointed under this Act by the local authority to make such appointments as are required under section 10(8);

"*building owner*"[72] means an owner of land who is desirous of exercising rights under this Act;

"foundation", in relation to a wall, means the solid ground or artificially formed support resting on solid ground on which the wall rests;

---

[70] *A Rent Act protected tenant is not an adjoining owner (Frances Holland School v Wasseff). However if they have been mistakenly treated as an owner the other party may be estopped from denying that fact.*

[71] *Next-door tenants may be "adjoining owners" even if they only rent a handful of rooms (Fillingham v Wood).*

[72] *"building owner" means all of the joint building owners acting together, not just one of them (Lehmann v Herman). A landlord that grants a tenant a licence to undertake works to a party structure is not "desirous of exercising rights" and is therefore not a building owner (Loost v Kremer).*

Section 20
continued

"*owner*" includes[73]—

(a) person in receipt of, or entitled to receive, the whole or part of the rents[74] or profits of land

(b) a person in possession of land, otherwise than as a mortgagee or as a tenant from year to year or for a lesser term or as a tenant at will;

(c) a purchaser of an interest in land under a contract for purchase or under an agreement for a lease, otherwise than under an agreement for a tenancy from year to year or for a lesser term;

"*party fence wall*" means a wall (not being part of a building) which stands on lands of different owners and is used or constructed to be used for separating such adjoining lands, but does not include a wall constructed on the land of one owner the artificially formed support of which projects into the land of another owner;

"*party structure*" means a party wall and also a floor partition or other structure separating buildings or parts of buildings approached solely by separate staircases or separate entrances;

---

[73] *This is not an exhaustive list and there may be other types of owner.*

[74] *A freehold owner that is only in receipt of a peppercorn rent may not be an owner for the purposes of this sub-section (Evelyn v Whichord).*

"*party wall*" means—

(a) a wall[75] which forms part of a building[76] and stands on lands of different owners[77] to a greater extent than the projection of any artificially formed support on which the wall rests; and

(b) so much of a wall not being a wall referred to in paragraph (a) above as separates buildings[78] belonging to different owners;

"*special foundations*" means foundations in which an assemblage of beams or rods is employed for the purpose of distributing any load; and

---

[75] *Two independent walls that touch, but are not bonded, are not a party wall (Thornton v Hunter).*

[76] *Where two or more terraced or semi-detached houses are built together, and sold off separately, the law will presume the wall dividing them is a party wall built equally on land belonging to both parties (Wiltshire v Sidford).*

[77] *If there is evidence of common user of a wall the law will presume, unless there is contrary evidence, that it is a party wall in equal ownership of the parties (Cubitt v Porter). It is possible for one party to obtain adverse possession of a party wall formerly in equal ownership (Prudential Assurance Co v Waterloo Real Estate Inc).*

[78] *A "type-b" wall is only a party wall to the extent that it is enclosed both sides, which seems* to be a question of user rather than title *(Knight v Pursell). The parts of the wall that do not separate two buildings are not party walls, and the building owner cannot do any works to those parts under this Act (Knight v Pursell). This includes a type-b parapet (London, Gloucester & North Hants Dairy Company v Morley and Lanceley).*

Section 20
continued

"*surveyor*" means any person[79] not being a party to the matter[80] appointed or selected under section 10 to determine disputes in accordance with the procedures set out in this Act.

---

[79] *A surveyor must be a natural person, and not a corporation (Loost v Kremer).*

[80] *Being the project architect does not prohibit a person from acting as surveyor (Loost v Kremer). The RICS Guidance Note suggests that a surveyor that has been involved in supervising the design is probably not appropriate.*

Section 21

Other statutory provisions

(1) The Secretary of State may by order amend or repeal any provision of a private of local Act passed before or in the same session as this Act, if it appears necessary or expedient to do so in consequence of this Act.

(2) An order made under subsection (1) may-

(a) Contain such savings or transitional provisions as the Secretary of state thinks fit;

(b) Make provision for different purposes

(3) The power to make an order under subsection (1) shall be exercisable by statutory instrument subject to annulment in pursuance of a resolution of either House of Parliament.

Section 22

Short title, commencement and extent

(1) This Act may be cited as the Party Wall etc. Act 1996

(2) This Act shall come into force in accordance with provision made by the secretary of State by order made by statutory instrument.

(3) An order under subsection (2) may-

(a) contain such saving or transitional provisions as the Secretary of State thinks fit;

(b) make different provision for different purposes

(4) This Act extends to England and Wales only.

PART II

CASE SUMMARIES

Adams v Marylebone Borough Council

Court: Court of Appeal

Statute: London Building Act 1894, s. 93(3)

Facts: Mrs Adams owned the lease of 33 John Street, Edgware. The Council owned the freehold of the next door property at 34.

In 1904 the Council started works without serving a party structure notice. Mrs Adams obtained an injunction stopping the works, as well as damages, including damages for loss of trade in her restaurant. The Council stopped works and served the correct notice.

The Court had awarded compensation for loss of trade until the date of service of the party structure notice. Mrs Adams asked the surveyors to award further damages for loss of business after the service of the party structure notice. The surveyors refused. Mrs Adams appealed.

Decision: The only right to compensation for adjoining owners was that set out in the 1894 Act. There was no "general" right to compensation.

Under the 1894 Act the only entitlement to compensation was in respect of physical damage. Adams was therefore not entitled to compensation for loss of business as the result of the works.

Comment: Under the 1894 Act the statutory indemnity applied only to excavations, but in the 1996 Act it applies to all works. This case is therefore likely to be decided differently today.

Andreae v Selfridge & Co Ltd

Court: Court of Appeal

Facts: Mrs Andrae operated a hotel from 119 - 121 Wigmore Street, London. This was part of the same island site that Selfridges were developing as a rolling project. Those works had continued throughout the night without interruption. Following complaints by Mrs Andrae the works paused between 10pm and 7am each night, but this was still unsatisfactory.

Mrs Andrae argued that those ongoing works constituted a nuisance to her business, and claimed damages of £4,500.

Decision: Adjoining owners must put up with a certain amount of discomfort. Temporary building works are a common and ordinary use of land and, therefore, if the building owner takes all reasonable steps to try and protect adjoining owners and/or occupiers he will not be liable even if, despite the pre-cautions, adjoining owners or occupiers are put to discomfort.

Apostal v Simons & Cave

Court: Court of Appeal

Statute: Law of Property Act 1925, s. 38

Facts: Apostal owned the freehold of 117 Hackney Road, London, E2. Simons owned the freehold of adjoining property at 1A Gorsuch Place. Cave was their tenant.

Cave stacked timber against the party wall which eventually damaged it so badly that a dangerous structure notice was served requiring the wall be demolished and rebuilt. Apostal brought a claim against Simons and Cave for the total cost of repairing the wall, on the basis that it was their fault. The lower Court dismissed the claim against Simons, but held that Cave & Co were liable for the damage and awarded the full cost of repair against them. Cave & Co appealed to the Court of Appeal.

Decision: The lower Court had been wrong to award the total cost of the repairing works.

Under s. 38 of the Law of Property Act 1925 the ownership in party walls were severed vertically on the boundary line and each owner having easements of user and support over the other half of the wall. As Apostal only owned one half of the wall, he can only recover on half of the cost or rebuilding it.

As to the other half, Apostal might have had a claim against Simons for interference with the easement of support, but this claim could only be brought against Simon, who was subject to the easement, and not a third party such as Cave.

Barry v Minturn

Court: House of Lords

Statute: London Building Act 1894, s. 88(1), s. 90(3)

Facts: Barry owned the freehold of 15 Chelsea Embankment, London, SW15. Minturn owned No. 14 next door.

At some point in the past a previous owner of No. 14 had added a rear extension, but the party wall of the extension was exposed to the elements. The wall was damp and allowed water to percolate into her basement.

Minturn wanted to undertake repairs to the party wall including the installation of a 2-inch damp proof membrane to Barry's side of the wall, which would keep the whole wall dry. Barry objected principally on the grounds that the work would cause unnecessary inconvenience to him.

Decision: Dampness of a wall did not, of itself, amount to a "defect" unless it rendered the wall less effective for the purposes for which it was intended to be used.

The previous history of the wall is immaterial when determining whether proposed works would be an unnecessary inconvenience. That the original construction might have caused the defect is irrelevant.

The surveyors must look only at the proposed works. If the works can be done in an equally effective way at no or modest extra cost, and this would result in less or no inconvenience or entry on to the adjoining land, then the surveyors ought to award those alternative works.

Bennett v Harrod's Stores Limited

Court: High Court

Statute: London Building Act 1894 s. 88(6), s. 90(1)

Facts: Bennett owned the lease of 40 & 42 Hans Crescent, the rear of which adjoined Harrods' land on the Brompton Road. They entered into a written agreement that allowed Harrods to raise the party wall between them.

Harrods raised the wall without serving notice on Bennett under the London Building Act 1894. Bennett complained because Harrods had raised the whole wall, but on Bennett's understanding of the agreement Harrods were only going to raise their half of it.

Bennett argued that the only right Harrods had to raise the whole width was under the 1894 Act, for which Harrods must first serve notice. As they had not served notice they were committing a trespass.

Decision: On the correct interpretation of the written agreement Harrods did have the right to raise the whole wall.

The Court also found that under the terms of the written agreement Harrods were entitled to exercise their rights under the 1894 Act without following the procedural requirements.

Bennett v Howell

Statute: London Building Act 1930, s. 5

Facts: Howell's surveyor drafted and served a party structure notice in the form then published by RIBA, but omitted to date the notice. Surveyors were duly appointed and an award was issued. Bennett appealed on the basis that because the notice was invalid, all that followed was invalid.

Decision: The failure to date the notice rendered it invalid. By reason of the notice being invalid, all that followed it was invalid, including the appointment of the surveyors and the award they made.

Breuer v Leccacorvi

Court: County Court

Statute: Party Wall etc. Act 1996, s. 7(2)

Facts: Breur undertook works to his property. Notices were served and an award permitting the works was made. The works caused damage to Leccacorvi's adjoining property. The quantum of those works was disputed.

Leccacorvi indicated that she might not undertake the works, but sell her property instead, although she had not yet made her mind up.

Breur argued that s. 11(8) required an award of the cost of the remedial works, but a claim under s. 7(2) should be subject to the common law principles – in particular that diminution in value, and not the cost of the remedial works, was the correct measure of loss.

Decision: Whilst s. 11(8) required that the costs of making good be awarded, compensation under s. 7(2) is subject to the general principles at common law, particularly where there was not decision as to whether the remedial works would be performed. In those circumstances there was a risk of over-compensation if the cost of the remedial works exceeded the diminution in value.

In this case damages would be awarded on the basis of diminution in value, not the cost of remedial works,

Burlington Property Company Limited v Odeon Theatres Limited

Court: Court of Appeal

Statute: London Building Act 1930, s. 114(7)

Facts: Odeon Theatres owned 33 Charing Cross Road. Burlington Property owned the adjoining premises at 35 Charing Cross Road. The flank wall of the theatre was a party wall owned by Odeon and Burlington in equal shares. On the other side of the wall was Hunt's Court, which although on Burlington Property's land, was subject to a public right of way.

Odeon wanted to demolish the wall and rebuild it with arches that would allow access to No. 33 from Hunt's Court. The surveyors made an award permitting the work. Burlington Properties appealed against it.

Decision: Odeon could only demolish and rebuild the party wall to substantially the same design as it was. They had no right to rebuild the wall to a different design. In permitting those works the surveyors had acted beyond their jurisdiction.

Capital & Leisure Hotels v Independent Estates Plc

Court: County Court

Statute: London Building Act 1930

Facts: Independent Estates were carrying out excavation works near Marylebone Station. Capital & Leisure were concerned their foundations would be put at risk, and requested £50,000 as security. Independent Estates refused. Capital issued proceedings

Decision: There was no serious risk of damage to the adjoining property. Security having been requested it was not open to the Court (or indeed the surveyors) to refuse to award it, although they could decide on the figure.

Comment: It seems that if security is requested it must be awarded, even if it is only nominal.

Chartered Society of Physiotherapy v Simmonds Church Smiles

Court: High Court

Statute: London Building Acts (Amendment) Act 1939, s. 55

Facts: The Society demolished and rebuilt a party wall having correctly followed the provisions of the 1939 Act. Some settlement damage occurred, and the third surveyor awarded that it was the result of the works by the Society. The Society appealed.

A number of issues arose, including the nature of a party wall award, and whether an appeal under the 1939 Act was by way of review or by way of rehearing.

Decision: The Court found that awards under the 1939 Act were not arbitration awards, and were not subject to the rules regarding arbitration; rather, they were in a category of their own, similar to an expert determination.

The Court also found that appeals under the 1939 Act were by way of rehearing, and not review.

Comment: The position with regards to appeals may have changed following a revision to the Civil Procedure Rules in October 2012.

Crofts v Haldane

Court: High Court

Statute: Metropolitan Building Act 1855, s. 83

Facts: Haldane raised a party wall having served notice and obtained an award under the Metropolitan Building Act 1855. The raised party wall interfered with Croft's right of light. Croft applied for an injunction.

Decision: Although a surveyors' award might authorise temporary interference with the adjoining owner's property rights, the surveyors have no jurisdiction to authorise permanent interference.

Judgment was entered for Crofts.

Crosby v Alhambra Company Limited

Court: High Court

Statute: London Building Act 1894, s. 5(32)

Facts: Alhambra owned the freehold of a theatre in Leicester Square. Crosby owned a lease of 28 Leicester Square next door, which in turn let the property to London County Council.

Alhambra wanted to undertake works to the party wall. They served the required notice on the Council, who consented. The works started in October 1906. In November 1906 Crosby found out about the works and requested permission to inspect them. Alhambra refused.

Crosby applied for an injunction stopping the works and argued that Alhambra had failed to comply with the 1894 Act in that Alhambra had not served notice on all the adjoining owners.

Decision: An injunction was granted. Building owners must serve notice on all owners of each separate leasehold and freehold.

However, where an individual leasehold or freehold was held by more than one person, notice may be served on only one of those joint owners.

Comment: Under s. 5(32) of the 1894 Act "adjoining owner" was defined as *"the owner or one of the owners"*, whereas the 1996 Act omits the phrase "*or one of the owners*" and so the case may be decided differently today.

Cubitt v Porter

Court: High Court

Facts: Cubitt's land was separated from Porter's land by a free-stranding wall. Both parties had exercised rights of user. Porter demolished the wall and rebuilt it to a greater height, then attached his cottage to it.

Cubitt alleged that this constituted a trespass.

Decision: Where there was evidence of common acts of user in a wall the law will presume that it is a party wall, in which case Porter had the right to demolish and rebuild the wall. No trespass had been committed.

Davis v Trustees of 2 Mulbery Walk

Court: County Court

Statute: Party Wall etc. Act 1996, s. 7(2)

Facts: In 1998, after complying with the Party Wall Act, the Trustees constructed a basement extension using reinforced underpinning. The underpinning over-spilled beyond the footings of the party wall with Davis' property, and were a trespass.

In 2008 Davis also constructed basement extension. As party of their works they cut away the overspill.

Davis made a claim against the Trustees under section 7(2) of the Party Wall Act for the costs resulting from cutting off the over-spilling foundations.

That claim was determined by an award by the third surveyor selected in relation to the 2008 works.

Decision: The award was invalid.

Compensation under s. 7(2) is only available to adjoining owners, not building owners. In the 2008 works Davis was a building owner, not an adjoining owner.

Evelyn v Whichcord

Statute: Metropolitan Building Act 1855, s. 51

Decision: A freehold owner who let their property to a tenant at a peppercorn rent was not an "owner" within the meaning of the Metropolitan Building Act 1855. A peppercorn was not included within the phrase "'*of the whole or of any part of the rents or profits of any land or tenement*' in section 3 of the 1855 Act.

Fillingham v Wood

Court: High Court

Statute: Metropolitan Building Act 1855, s. 3, s. 82.

Facts: Wood owned the freehold of 40 Margaret Street, London. Fillingham owned a 3 year lease of various rooms in the ground and first floors of the adjoining property at No 41.

Wood wanted to undertake works to the party wall which included laying open some of the rooms that Fillingham leased. Wood served notice on Fillingham's head landlord, but not Fillingham himself. Upon expiry of the notice Wood started works, including laying open Fillingham's bedroom.

Fillingham issued proceedings for an injunction on the basis he had not been served with the required notice under the Metropolitan Building Act 1855.

Wood argued, among other issues, that Fillingham was not entitled to notice of the works because he was only in occupation of some of the adjoining property, not all of it.

Decision: Anyone who met the description of an adjoining owner was entitled to receive notice no matter how small their interest in the adjoining land. Fillingham was an adjoining owner, and was therefore entitled to notice before the works recommenced.

An injunction was granted.

Frances Holland School v Wassef

Court: County Court

Statute: London Building Acts (Amendment) Act 1939, s. 55

Facts: The School wanted to undertake works to a party wall as well as adjacent excavation works to their property at 21 - 23 Graham Terrace, London. They served notice on Wassef, who occupied No 25 on a Rent Act protected tenancy. An award was issued authorising the works. After the works a third surveyor published an award dealing with remedial works for damage to No. 25.

Wassef's surveyor also issued a further *ex parte* award. The school appealed that award on, among other grounds, that having reviewed the position, Wassef was not in fact an "adjoining owner" within the meaning of the 1939 Act.

Decision: The Court found that Wassef was not an "owner" within the meaning of the Act, but by reason of the shared mistake that he was, and their reliance that on it, it would be unconscionable to now hold that the whole process was invalid.

Estoppel by convention therefore applied, and the School was prevented from arguing that the awards that had already been made were invalid on this point.

The estoppel ended when the mistake was discovered, and would not apply to future awards.

Freetown Limited v Assethold Limited

Court: Court of Appeal

Statute: Party Wall etc, Act 1996, s.15

Facts: Freetown owned the freehold of 12 Westport Street, London. Assethold held a long lease of the adjoining property at 14 Westport Street. Freehold wanted to undertake works to the party wall and the relevant notices were served. On Friday 22 July 2011 the third surveyor made an award, and on that day or the day after (Saturday 23) he posted it to the parties.

Freetown appealed that award on 08 August 2011. Assethold argued that the 14 day time limit in section 10(17) of the Party Wall etc. Act 1996 ran from the date the award was posted, which meant that the appeal had to have been issued on or before Thursday 4 or Friday 5 August 2011. As it was issued on Monday 8 August the appeal was out of time.

The County Court and, on appeal, the High Court, found that the award was deemed served on the date on which it was posted to the parties. Freetown appealed to the Court of Appeal.

Decision: The deemed service provisions in s. 15 of the Party Wall etc Act 1996 were subject to section 7 of the Interpretation Act 1978. An award was deemed served when it would have been received in the ordinary course of post unless the contrary is proved.

Gyle-Thompson & Others v Wall Street Properties Limited

Court: High Court

Statute: London Building Acts (Amendment) Act 1939, s.46, s. 47, s. 55

Facts: Wall Street owned the freehold of a warehouse at 57 – 63 Old Church Street, Chelsea. The flank wall of the warehouse also formed the rear garden wall of the houses at 43 – 53 Paulton's Square. It was assumed that this wall was in the sole ownership of Wall Street.

Wall Street demolished all of the warehouse save for the flank wall. During the works a plaque was discovered indicating that it was in fact a party wall. Wall Street then served a notice under the 1939 Act.

That notice, and subsequent award, was served on the adjoining owners' surveyor, and not the adjoining owners. Wall Street started the works as soon as the 14 day appeal period had run. Gyle-Thompson and the other adjoining owners applied for an injunction to stop the works.

Wall Street argued, among other matters, that because the 14 day appeal period had run the adjoining owners could not challenge the award

Decision: An injunction was granted.

The 1939 Act gave a building owner the right to raise a party wall, but did not grant the right to reduce it in height. The award was therefore bad in law.

Although the 14 day time period had run, this time period only applied to a valid award made within the surveyors' jurisdiction. Here, reducing the height of the wall was not within the surveyor's jurisdiction, and so the award was not valid.

Although the above grounds were sufficient to grant the injunction, the Court also considered the procedural irregularities; that the notice and the award were served on the adjoining owners' surveyor (and not the adjoining owners), and that the adjoining owners' surveyor had not been formally appointed in writing for the purposes of the 1939 Act.

The Court held that each of these issues would render the award invalid. The Court suggested to surveyors that they should ask for each other's letter of appointment to check that they were properly appointed.

Hobbs, Hart & Co v Grover

Court: Court of Appeal

Statute: London Building Act 1894, 90(1)

Facts: Hobbs owned 76 Cheapside in London. Grover owned number 75. The properties were separated by a party wall. Grover wanted to demolish and rebuild 75, and served notice to that effect.

Hobbs claimed the notice was invalid, as it did not contain "the nature and particulars of the proposed works" as required by section 90(1) of the London Building Act 1894, and applied for an injunction restraining the works.

Decision: The notice was not valid.

A party structure notice must be so clear and intelligible that the adjoining owner can judge whether he should consent to the works and what (if any) counter-notice he might serve, especially in respect of the adjoining owners right to require the building owner to undertake works.

J. Jarvis & Sons Ltd v Baker

Court: High Court

Statute: London Building Acts (Amendment) Act 1939, s.58

Facts: Mrs Baker undertook works to a party wall authorised by an award. That award required the adjoining owner, Mr Benkert, to pay half of the cost of the works. The works were undertaken and completed by Baker's builder, Jarvis. Baker paid her half of the costs.

Baker's surveyor omitted to serve an account on Mr Benkert within two months of completion of the works. Baker refused to pay Jarvis the remaining half on the basis that it was Benkert's responsibility.

Jarvis sued Baker on the basis that the contract was with her, notwithstanding any arrangements there may be with a third party. Baker issue a third party claim against Benkert

Decision: The Court found Baker liable for the fees in the main claim against her by the builder, Jarvis.

In the third party claim the Court found Benkert was liable under the award, notwithstanding that an account had not been served on him.

Comment: This decision conflicts with Spiers & Sons Ltd v Troup where an account was held not to be valid if served out of time.

Jolliffe v Woodhouse

Court: Court of Appeal

Statute: Metropolitan Building Act 1855, s. 85

Facts: Jolliffe was the tenant of 17 Coronet Street, Hoxton. Woodhouse owned the freehold of 19 Coronet Street. Woodhouse wanted to demolish and rebuild No. 17, but without demolishing the party wall.

During the works it was discovered that the party wall was of insufficient strength to support the new building. Woodhouse served notice on Jolliffe to demolish and rebuild. Surveyors were appointed, and an award was published.

The works to the wall took 7 months. Joliffe complained that this was too long to be considered reasonable interference, and issued proceedings for Woodhouse's breach of his duty not to cause unreasonable inconvenience to Jolliffe.

Woodhouse argued that he was not liable because, although there had been delays, he had employed competent architects and workmen and had delegated his duty to them.

Decision: The Court found that Woodhouse could not delegate his responsibility not to cause inconvenience to his contractors; it remained personal to Jolliffe.

The Court held that 7 months was too long to be exposed to construction works, and so Woodhouse had breached his duty not to cause unreasonable inconvenience.

Kaye v Lawrence

Court: High Court

Statute: Party Wall etc. Act 1996, s. 12

Facts: Lawrence was the owner of 124 Panorama Road in Poole. Mr Kaye owned the adjoining property at 126. Lawrence served notice in relation to proposed excavation works. Mr Lawrence requested security for expenses under section 12 of the 1996 Act.

The third surveyor issued an award refusing Mr Kaye's request on the basis that security was only available under section 12 if works were being undertaken on or to the adjoining owner's land. Mr Kaye appealed.

An additional issue arose as to whether the High Court had jurisdiction to deal with an appeal under section 10(17) of the 1996 Act.

Decision: The 1996 Act operated as a wholesale replacement of any common law rights. There was therefore no distinction between works on the building owner's land or the adjoining owner's land and therefore it was open to the adjoining owner to request security.

On the additional issue it was held appeals under the Act must be issued in the County Court, although they could be transferred to the High Court later.

Kelliher v Ash Estates

Court: County Court

Statute: Party Wall etc. Act 1996, s. 2(2)(n) & s. 7(2)

Facts: Ash commenced works, including removal of the plaster to their side of the party wall with percussive tools and excavations for pilling without serving notice.

Ash's contractors failed to follow designs which resulted in massive cracking damage being caused to Kelliher's property. There was a 12 week delay whilst the foundations were resigned as a result.

The third surveyor declined to award damages caused by the removal of plaster because it was not "*work executed in pursuance of*" the 1996 Act. He also refused to award damages for loss of earnings.

Decision: Whether removing plaster "*work executed in pursuance of*" the 1996 Act depends on the method used. Removal with manual tools is not, but removal using percussive tools is.

Loss of earnings is, in principle, recoverable under the statutory indemnity but the claim was not made out on the facts of this case. It is also possible to recover damages for loss of amenity.

The 12 week delay was unreasonable and so would give rise to a claim for breach of the duty not to cause unreasonable inconvenience.

Knight v Pursell

Court: High Court

Statute: Metropolitan Building Act 1855, s. 3

Facts: Knight owned a lease of 6 and 7 Surrey Row, London. Pursell owned the freehold of adjoining land at 172 Blackfriars Road.

Knight owned a freestanding brick wall that separated his land from Pursell's, and which was entirely on Knight's land.

Pursell erected a lean-to structure against the wall. Shortly after Knight erected a number of closets and small lean-tos along various points of the wall so that at some parts the wall separated Knight's enclosures from Pursell's.

The wall was in poor repair. Pursell wanted to demolish and rebuild it, and served the required notice. Knight objected and applied for an injunction. Knight argued that it could not be a party wall unless both owners had some property in it.

Decision: A building owner does not have to have any property in the wall before they can exercise any of their rights. It is the way in which the wall is used that makes it a party wall.

However, those rights only apply in as far as it is a party wall. To the extent that not all of the wall separated two buildings it was not a party wall, and so the building owner could not exercise any rights over those parts of it.

Leadbetter v Marylebone Corporation [No. 1]

Court: Court of Appeal

Statute: London Building Act 1894, s.91

Facts: Leadbetter owned the freehold of 33 John Street, Near Edgeware Road. Marylebone owned the freehold of No. 34 next-door. The properties were separated by a party wall. Leadbetter wanted to demolish and rebuild his property, including demolishing and rebuilding the party wall.

Notice was served in 1902, and an award made. That award purported to give Marylebone the right to raise the party wall at any point in the future. The works were completed by Leadbetter.

In 1904 Marylebone started works to raise the party wall without serving notice. They argued that the original award authorised the works. Leadbetter objected because he had not received notice and applied for an interim injunction to stop the works, which was granted. Marylebone appealed the injunction to the Court of Appeal.

Decision: The surveyors had a strictly limited jurisdiction to deal with the works identified in the party structure notice only. They had no jurisdiction to deal with separate future works. The part of the 1902 award that authorised the works was invalid.

The appeal was dismissed and the injunction continued in force.

Leadbetter v Marylebone Corporation [No. 2]

Court: Court of Appeal

Statute: London Building Act 1894, s.90

Facts: Following the earlier decision Marylebone served a party structure notice. However, an award had still not be made six months later.

Leadbetter sought the removal of the earlier works because, the party structure notice having expired, Marylebone was now in breach of the injunction.

Decision: The Court found that the six month time for commencing works in s. 90 (now twelve months in the 1996 Act) applied only where the adjoining owner had consented to the works and were proceeding on the notice only.

Where the adjoining owner had dissented to the notice and the matter was being dealt with by the surveyors this limitation period did not apply.

Comment: This case is the rational for surveyors including a time period (usually 12 months) in their awards. The validity of such a clause has not been tested.

Lehmann v Herman

Court:	Court of Appeal
Statute:	London Building Act 1930, s. 5
Facts:	Mr and Mrs Lehmann owned the freehold of 35 Reddington Road, London. Mr and Mrs Herman owned a long lease of Flat A in no 33 Reddington Road. Mr Herman served a party structure notice in respect of demolishing and rebuilding the party wall. The notice was served on behalf of Mr Herman only, and not Mrs Herman. Mr and Mrs Lehmann argued that the notice was invalid, and applied to the Court for a declaration to that effect
Decision:	The Court found that a notice served by one of two or more joint tenants is not valid, because the term "building owner" means all of the building owners acting together, and not just one of them.

London, Gloucester & North Hants Dairy Company v Morley and Lanceley

Court: High Court

Statute: London Building Act 1930, s. 5, s. 58

Facts: The Dairy was a tenant of land in Lambeth which included a wall in their sole ownership that had originally been free-standing, but had subsequently been enclosed upon both sides, save for a small parapet on top. The adjoining land was owned by Morley and Lanceley.

Morley and Lanceley served notice to raise the wall and an award authorising the works was made. The Dairy appealed to the County Court, which found that the award was invalid on the basis that it was only a party wall to the extent it was enclosed upon, and as the parapet was not enclosed upon, Morley and Lanceley could not raise it.

Morley and Lanceley appealed to the High Court.

Decision: As the parapet was not enclosed upon both sides it was not a party wall and belonged solely to the Dairy.

Morley and Lanceley therefore had no right to raise it.

Loost v Kremer

Court: County Court

Statute: London Building Act 1930, s. 5
London Building Act (Amendment) Act 1939, s. 44

Facts: Kremer owned the leasehold of the top flat at 37 Upper Addison Gardens, London. Mrs Bartholomew owned the freehold. Mr and Mrs Loost owned the whole freehold of the adjoining no. 36.

Kremer wanted to convert the loft space above his flat. He obtained a licence for the works from Mrs Bartholomew as well as a deed of variation of his lease bringing the party wall into his demise. He then served a party structure notice.

Mr and Mrs Loost objected on the basis that:-

(a) The notice was invalid as it had only been served by Mr Kremer when it should also have been served on behalf of Mrs Bartholomew, as she was also a building owner

(b) That the deed of variation was a sham, and that Mr Kremer did not really have any interest in the party wall;

(c) That the appointment of Mr Kremer's project architect as his party wall surveyor was not valid, as there was a conflict of interest between those two roles.

These issues were referred to the third surveyor, who found against Mr and Mrs Loost who then appealed to the County Court.

In addition to the above issues, Mr and Mrs Loost also argued that the third surveyor had no jurisdiction to deal with the above three issues as they were matters of law, and were the sole jurisdiction of the Courts.

Decision: Mr and Mrs Loost's appeal was dismissed

On the first issue, Mrs Bartholomew was not a building owner within the meaning of the Act. She was not undertaking the construction work herself, and the mere fact that she granted the licence and executed the deed did not mean that she was "desirous" of the work within the relevant definition.

On the second issue, ownership or otherwise of the wall was irrelevant. The two tests were whether it was a party wall, and whether Mr Kremer was a building owner. Provided those two tests were met, which they were, Mr Kremer had the right to undertake the works.

On the third issue, being the project architect does not disqualify someone from being a party wall surveyor. The Court also found that a surveyor must be a natural person, and could not be a company or a firm.

On the fourth issue, although they were matters of law, the third surveyor could not have made an award without dealing with them. Surveyors can deal with matters of law if they so choose (provided that the issues arise within their jurisdiction under the Act) but that decision is not final; it can be challenged in the Courts.

Marchant v Capital & Counties plc

Court: Court of Appeal

Statute: London Building Acts (Amendment) Act 1939, s. 55

Facts: Marchant's property was built against a wall in Capital' sole ownership.

Capital later demolished their warehouse the other side leaving their side of the wall exposed to the weather.

At the time of demolition a party wall award was made that required Capital to "Maintain the exposed face of the party wall in a weatherproof condition". Capital failed to do so, resulting in damp penetrating through the wall and into Marchant's property.

Marchant issued proceedings. Capital argued that it was beyond the power of the surveyors to impose an indefinite obligation.

Decision: The surveyors did have the power to impose ongoing and indefinite obligations, and in particular an ongoing obligation to provide weatherproofing.

Mason v Fulham Corporation

Court: High Court

Statute: London Building Act 1894, s. 95, s.99

Facts: Mason wanted to raise the party wall between his property and the Fulham Library. A notice was served and an award was made. That award stated that the Corporation would have the right to use the party wall at any time upon payment of one half of the cost of building the wall. Mason subsequently sold the property.

In 1908 Fulham served a notice on the new owner of Mason's house, Sir Edward Galsworthy, stating their intention to enclose upon the wall. Notices were served and an award made which required the Corporation to pay to Sir Edward one half of the cost of the wall, which they did.

Mason later found out about the payment, and issued proceedings against the Corporation. He argued that the payment should be made to the person who raised the wall originally, not the person who may own it for the time being.

Decision: Mason's claim was dismissed.

Compensation payable for subsequent use of the works is to be paid to the building owner at the time the use is made; not to the building owner who originally constructed the wall.

Observatory Hill Limited v Camtel Investments SA

Court: High Court

Statute: London Building Act (Amendment) Act 1939

Facts: Observatory wanted to undertake works under the London Building Act (Amendment) Act 1939. Notices were served and an award made. That award required Observatory to make good any damage to Camtel's land, or in default of making good, authorised Camtel to enter on to Observatory's land to undertake the works at Observatory's expense.

Camtel applied to register the award at Land Registry as a caution against Observatory's title.

Decision: The application was dismissed.

Adjoining owners' rights arising from an award are not capable of registration as a caution.

Comment: Cautions were replaced by Unilateral and Agreed Notices under the Land Registration Act 2002.

Patel v Peters

Court: Court of Appeal

Statute: Party Wall etc. Act 1996, s. 10(7)

Facts: Peters' surveyor served a request under section 10(7) of the 1996 Act asking Patel's surveyor to review his timesheets when determining his fees.

Patel's surveyor replied, outside the 10 day period, refusing to review the time sheets and proposed taking a global approach to fees instead.

Peters' surveyor took that as failing to act effectively and made an award *ex parte*. Patel appealed.

Decision: To act effectively all a surveyor need do is reply to the request engaging with the subject matter of the request and setting out his position. If he does so then the other surveyor may not act *ex parte*.

If a defaulting surveyor acts effectively after the expiry to the 10 day period, but before the other surveyor has acted, this will bring to an end the power to make an *ex parte* award.

Prudential Assurance Co Limited v Waterloo Real Estate Inc

Court: Court of Appeal

Statute: Limitation Act 1980, s. 15(1), s. 17, Schedule 1

Facts: A 30 metre party wall sat equally astride land owned by Prudential and land owned by Waterloo. 7 metres of this wall formed the flank wall of the Normandie Hotel on Waterloo's land. A smaller portion also formed the flank wall of a pub on Prudential's land called the Pakenham Tavern. The Pakenham was demolished in 1957.

Since then the owners of Waterloo's land had treated the wall as their own. They had cleaned it, repaired it, maintained it, and granted leases to their tenants including repairing covenants relating to the wall. They therefore claimed adverse possession of the whole wall.

Decision: Waterloo's conduct in respect of the wall clearly demonstrated the necessary intention to possess the wall. They had therefore acquired adverse possession of the whole wall.

Re Stone & Hastie

Court: Court of Appeal

Statute: London Building Act 1894, s. 95, s. 99

Facts: Stone owned the freehold of 6 Queen Street, London. Hastie owned the leasehold of 7 Queen Street. Prior to the grant of that lease Hastie's landlord had raised the party wall. Stone later made use of the raised section.

The surveyors appointed for those later works made an award requiring Stone to pay the contribution for the cost of using the raised portion of the wall to Hastie, rather than Hastie's landlord.

Stone did not pay, so Hastie applied to the Court to enforce the award. Stone argued that the award was invalid because the compensation should have been payable to his landlord, who raised the wall, rather than Hastie.

Decision: The Claim was dismissed, The right to receive compensation is not transferred on the grant of a lease. The compensation was therefore not payable to Hastie, but to his landlord.

Reading v Barnard

Court: High Court

Statute: London Building Act 1774, s. 41

Facts: Reading demolished and rebuilt a defective party wall that divided Reading's land from Barnard's land. Reading then served an account on Barnard for half the cost of rebuilding the wall.

The 1774 Act sets out maximum amounts per rod that could be charged.

Barnard refused to pay on the basis that the account was defective; it claimed more than the 1774 Act allowed Reading to recover.

Decision: The account contained enough information about the quantities used to enable the total amount due to be calculated under the 1774 Act.

It was not invalidated simply because it claimed more than the 1774 Act would allow.

Reeves v Blake

Court: Court of Appeal

Statute: Party Wall etc. Act 1996, s. 10

Facts: Blake served notices under s. 1(5) and s. 6 regarding works. Blake argued that the notice under s. 1(5) was invalid. The surveyors determined that the first notice was not valid, but the s. 6 notice was valid and authorised those works. Blake instructed the contractors to start works. Reeves disagreed on the basis that an additional award was required before works could commence, and instructed her solicitors to prepare an application for an injunction.

Reeves' solicitors wrote to Blake stating that unless Blake gave an undertaking to stop works they would issue the proceedings. Blake gave the undertaking, and proceedings were not issued.

The surveyors issued an addendum award that, among other matters, required Blake to pay for the costs of Reeves' abortive application for an injunction. Blake appealed.

Decision: Proceedings for an injunction to enforce common law rights fell outside the Party Wall Act 1996, and so were not within the surveyors' jurisdiction.

The award was therefore incorrect, the appeal allowed and the award amended.

Riley Gowler Ltd v National Heart Hospital

Court: Court of Appeal

Statute: London Building Acts (Amendment) Act 1939, s. 55(n)

Facts: The third surveyor wrote to the parties on 27 May 1968 stating that his award was ready. On 28 May Riley Gowler paid the third surveyor's fees and collected the award that day. The third surveyor posted the award to the Hospital, which arrived on 29 May.

Riley issued an appeal. The Hospital argued that the appeal was out of time. Riley had issued the appeal within 14 days of when the hospital received it on 29 May, but not within 14 days of when Riley received it, on 28 May.

Decision: The award was served on Riley when they actually received it, irrespective of when the Hospital may have received it.

Seeff v Ho

Court:	Court of Appeal
Statute:	Party Wall etc. Act 1996, s. 3(3)
Facts:	Mr and Mrs Ho wanted to undertake works to 314 Whitchurch Lane, Edgware, London. Mr and Mrs Seeff owned 316. Before the works started Mrs Ho and Mrs Seeff had a conversation over the garden fence during which Mrs Seeff had given consent to the works. Mr and Mrs Ho started works without serving notice as they (mistakenly) believed the wall between the properties was not a party wall. Part of those works committed a trespass to no 316. Shortly after the works were completed Mr and Ms Seeff applied for an injunction ordering the removal of the offending works. Mr and Mrs Ho argued that the earlier oral agreement overrode the requirement for notice
Decision:	An oral agreement to the works does not override the requirement for notice. Any agreement must be in writing. The works were therefore unlawful.

Selby v Whitbread & Co

Court: High Court

Statute: London Building Act 1894

Facts: Selby owned the freehold of 11 Royal Mint Street, London. Whitbread & Co owned the Rising Sun pub at no. 12. Whitbread wanted to demolish and rebuild number 12.

Whitbread obtained consent from the licensing justices, but that consent came with a condition that the new pub be set back from the street to provide a wider footpath. Whitbread entered into an agreement with London County Council that the strip of land to the front of the new pub would be transferred to the Council, and dedicated as a highway.

Whitbread then served a party structure notice on Selby, and an award was made authorising the works. The Rising Sun was demolished in March 1915 and, in accordance with the agreement, on April 1915 the strip of land was transferred to the Council. The works were completed in August 1915 and the new Rising Sun pub had opened.

In January 1916 the lack of support to the part of the party wall that was exposed when the Rising Sun was set back was causing damage. Selby's surveyor and the third surveyor issued an addendum award requiring Whitbread to erect a pier on the land they had transferred to the Council to support the exposed wall. Whitbread did not appeal the award, or comply with it. Selby issued proceedings to enforce the addendum award.

Whitbread argued that, as they had transferred the relevant land to the Council, they were no longer building owners within the meaning of the 1894 Act;

following *Mason v Fulham Corporation* the Council were now the relevant building owner, and the award should have been made against them.

Whitbread also argued that the surveyors' tribunal had no authority to make an addendum award because the first award had dealt with the issues in dispute exhaustively.

Decision: The Court found that Whitbread was liable as building owner irrespective of the fact that the relevant land had been transferred to the Council. Whilst *Mason v Fulham Corporation* was correct that benefits, such as the right to receive compensation, was transferred to a new owner liabilities such as the obligation here to remedy a withdrawal of support, was not transferred; it remained with the building owner that did the work.

On the second issue the Court found that the surveyors' tribunal retains the ability to make further addendum awards where required.

Rashid v Sharif

Court: Court of Appeal

Statute: Party Wall Act 1996

Facts: Sharif demolished a party fence wall and rebuilt it as a party wall astride the boundary line and incorporated the new wall into his new "shed". Sharif did not serve notice under the Party Wall Act.

Rashid issued proceedings alleging the rebuilt party wall was a trespass of 9 inches into his land, and sought an injunction requiring it to be removed.

The County Court found that there was a trespass and granted the injunction. Sharif appealed to the Court of Appeal.

Decision: The Court of Appeal found that, because Sharif has now served notices under the 1996 Act he had no right to place part of the wall on Rashid's land. To that extend it was a trespass.

The Court of Appeal held the injunction was disproportionate to the trespass, set it aside and replaced it with an award of damages of £300.

Thornton v Hunter

Court: High Court

Statute: London Building Act 1894

Facts: Thornton owned 63 High Street, Clapham. Hunter owned the freehold of number 65. The properties were separated by two independent half-brick (4 ½ inch) walls. The two walls touched, but were not bonded.

Thornton demolished his property, including his skin of the wall. He erected a shore to support Hunter's wall, but it was ineffective and the next day part of it collapsed. Hunter immediately started to build a single skin replacement party wall with footings on Thornton's side of the boundary. Thornton issued proceedings.

Decision: The original wall was not a party wall, but two separate walls. As it was not originally a party wall the London Building Act 1894 Act did not apply.

As a result, Hunter did not have the right to place any footings on Thornton's land.

Wiltshire v Sidford

Court: High Court

Facts: Wiltshire & Sidford owned two semi-detached houses.

.

Sidford demolished his house and half of the party wall separating them. He then enclosed his new house on the remaining half of the wall.

Wiltshire argued that this was a trespass because the whole of the party wall was within his ownership.

Decision: Where two or more houses are constructed together, then sold off separately, the law presumes that the wall dividing them is a party wall built equally on land belonging to each property.

Zissis v Lukomski

Court: Court of Appeal

Statute: Party Wall etc. Act 1996, s. 10(17)

Facts: Zissis owned 8 Birkdale Road in Acton. Lukomski owned the adjoining property No. 10. In 2003 Zissis wished to undertake works. Notices were served, and an award duly made authorising the works, but it did not deal with the fees of the adjoining owner's surveyor, Mr Carter.

Mr Carter issued an award requiring Zissis to pay him £15,825 plus VAT. Zissis issued an appeal under section 10(17) using the procedure in Part 8 of the Civil Procedure Rules. Mr Carter applied to enforce his award using the summary procedure under rule 70.5 of the Civil Procedure Rules.

Decision: Zissis' appeal was procedurally incorrect. An appeal under section 10(17) of the 1996 Act must be made under Part 52 of the Civil Procedure Rules, not Part 8.

The enforcement application was also incorrect. Awards under the 1996 Act cannot be enforced using the summary procedure in CPR 70.5

PART III

PRECEDENTS

Precedent 1A

Party Wall etc. Act 1996, section 1(2)

LINE OF JUNCTION NOTICE
NEW PARTY WALL

To: [*INSERT NAME*] of [*INSERT ADDRESS*]

1. This notice is served under section 1(2) of the Party Wall etc. Act 1996 ("the Act").

2. I am the owner of [*INSERT ADDRESS*] which adjoins your property at [*INSERT ADDRESS*].

3. I **REQUEST** your written permission to build a new wall as a party wall astride the boundary between our properties.

4. The proposed works are show in the attached plan[s].

5. If you do not provide your written permission within 14 days of service of this notice the wall will be built wholly on my land up to, but not across, the boundary line and under section 1(6) of the Act I intend to put projecting footings and/or foundations under your land.

6. I intend to start works on [*INSERT DATE*] or sooner with your written agreement.

Signed:-

.... Dated:

[*INSERT NAME*]

Precedent 1B

Party Wall etc. Act 1996, section 1(5)

LINE OF JUNCTION NOTICE
NEW BOUNDARY WALL

To: [*INSERT NAME*] of [*INSERT ADDRESS*]

1. This notice is served under section 1(5) of the Party Wall etc. Act 1996 ("the Act").

2. I am the owner of [*INSERT ADDRESS*] which adjoins your property at [*INSERT ADDRESS*].

3. I **GIVE NOTICE** of my intention to build a new wall wholly on my land up to, but not across, the boundary line and under section 1(6) of the Act I intend to put protecting footings and/or foundations under your land.

4. The proposed works are shown in the attached plan[s].

5. I intend to start works on [*INSERT DATE*] or sooner with your written agreement.

Signed:-

.... Dated:
[*INSERT NAME*]

Precedent 3A

Party Wall etc. Act 1996, section 3

PARTY STRUCTURE NOTICE

To: [*INSERT NAME*] of [*INSERT ADDRESS*]

1. This notice is served under section 3 of the Party Wall etc. Act 1996 ("the Act").

2. I am the owner of [*INSERT ADDRESS*] which adjoins your property at [*INSERT ADDRESS*].

3. I **GIVE NOTICE** that in accordance with my rights under section 2 of the Act I intent to carry out the following building works:

    a. [*LIST THE NOTIFIABLE WORKS*]

4. The proposed works [*do*][*do not*] include special foundations.

5. The proposed works are shown in the attached plans.

6. I intend to start works on [*INSERT DATE*] or sooner with your written agreement.

7. If you do not provide your written permission within 14 days of service of this notice a "deemed dispute" will have arisen

Signed:-

.... Dated:

[*INSERT NAME*]

Precedent 4A

Party Wall etc. Act 1996, section 4(1)(a)

COUNTER-NOTICE REQUIRING ADDITIONAL WORKS TO A PARTY STRUCTURE

To: [*INSERT NAME*]

1. This counter-notice is served under section 4 of the Party Wall etc. Act 1996 ("the Act").

2. On [*INSERT DATE*] you served a notice under section 3 of the Act ("the Notice").

3. **I REQUIRE** that you build into the wall to which the Notice relates the chimney copings, breasts, jambs, flues, piers, recesses and other works as set out in the plans, sections and particulars which are attached to this counter-notice.

Signed:-

.... Dated:

[*INSERT NAME*]

Precedent 4B

<u>Party Wall etc. Act 1996, section 4(1)(b)</u>

COUNTER-NOTICE REQUIRING ADDITIONAL WORKS TO SPECIAL FOUNDATIONS

To: [*INSERT NAME*]

1. This counter-notice is served under section 4 of the Party Wall etc. Act 1996 ("the Act").

2. On [*INSERT DATE*] you served a notice under section 6 of the Act ("the Notice").

3. On [*INSERT DATE*] I consented in writing to special foundations being placed upon my land.

4. **I REQUIRE** that the said special foundations:-

   a. Be placed to a depth greater than that specified in the Notice; and/or

   b. Be constructed of sufficient strength to bear the load to be carried by my intended building.

   in accordance with the plans, sections and particulars which are attached to this counter-notice.

Signed:-

.... Dated:

[*INSERT NAME*]

Precedent 6A

<u>Party Wall etc. Act 1996, section 6</u>

NOTICE OF ADJACENT EXCAVATIONS

To: [*INSERT NAME*] of [*INSERT ADDRESS*]

1. This notice is served under section 6 of the Party Wall etc. Act 1996 ("the Act").

2. I am the owner of [*INSERT ADDRESS*] which adjoins your property at [*INSERT ADDRESS*].

3. I **GIVE NOTICE** that in accordance with my rights under section 6 of the Act I intent to [excavate and] build within [*three*] **OR** [*six*] metres of your building and to a lower level than the bottom of your foundations [*measured by a 45 degree line*] by carrying out the works detailed below:

    a. [*LIST THE NOTIFIABLE WORKS*]

4. The accompanying plans and sections show the site of the proposed building and the excavation depth.

5. I [do not] propose to underpin or otherwise strengthen in order to safeguard the foundations of your property.

6. I intend to start works on [*INSERT DATE*] or sooner with your written agreement.

Signed:-

.... Dated:

[*INSERT NAME*]

Precedent 7A

Party Wall etc. Act 1996, section 7(4)

DEED CONSENTING TO SPECIAL FOUNDATIONS IN EXCHANGE FOR WAIVER OF S. 11 CONTRIBUTION FOR LATER USE

THIS DEED is made this [ ] day of [ ]

BETWEEN:-

(1) [*INSERT NAME*] ("*the Building Owner*") of [INSERT ADDRESS] ("*the Property*"); and

(2) [*INSERT NAME*] ("*the Adjoining Owner*") of [INSERT ADDRESS] ("*the Adjoining Property*")

BACKGROUND

1. The [freehold][leasehold] of the Property is vested in the Building Owner and is registered at HM Land Registry under title number [*INSERT TITLE NUMBER*].

2. The [freehold][leasehold] of the Adjoining Property is vested in the Adjoining Owner and is registered at HM Land Registry under title number [*INSERT TITLE NUMBER*].

AGREED TERMS

1. Interpretation

The following definitions apply in this Deed:

1996 Act: The Party Wall etc. Act 1996 as amended from time to time or any other legislation that may replace it.

Plan: The Plan attached to this Deed.

Special Foundations: Special Foundations within the meaning of section 20 of the 1996 Act.

Notifiable Work: The work set out in the notice served by the Building Owner under section 6 of the Party Wall etc. Act 1996 dated [*INSERT DATE*]

2. Consent of Adjoining Owner

2.1 Subject to the other provisions of this clause and in consideration of the Building Owner's release contained in clause 3 the Adjoining Owner **HEREBY CONSENTS** to the placing of the Special Foundations on the Adjoining Property as set out in the Plan without any variations whether material or not.

2.2 If the Building Owner does not commence the Notifiable Work within 12 months of the date of this Deed the above consent shall expire and the Building Owner may not place Special Foundations on the Adjoining Property save by further written consent.

3 Release by Building Owner

3.1 In consideration of the consent contained in clause 2 above the Building Owner **HEREBY RELEASES** and forever discharges any and all claims to a contribution to the cost of the Works from the Adjoining Owner under section 11(11) of the 1996 Act.

3.2 For the avoidance of doubt the release in clause 3.1 applies only to a contribution due under section 11(11) of the 1996 Act and does not affect any other rights or liabilities of either party under the 1996 Act.

3.3 The release in clause 3.1 is given by the Building Owner with the intent that it will bind himself his successors in title and any persons in future having or claiming title to the Property and that it will enure for the benefit of the Adjoining Owner and his successors in title and any persons in future having or claiming title to the Adjoining Property.

4 Registration at HM Land Registry

Within 7 days of the date of this Deed the Building Owner will register this Deed at HM Land Registry against the title of the Property and the Adjoining Property for which purpose the parties hereby consent to the registration of this deed against their respective titles.

.

Signed as a Deed }
by the Building Owner }
In the presence of } ....

Signature: ....
Name: ....
Address: ....
....
....
Occupation: ....

Signed as a Deed }
by the Adjoining Owner }
In the presence of } ....

Signature: ....
Name: ....
Address: ....
....
....
Occupation: ....

Precedent 8A

Party Wall etc. Act 1996, section 8

NOTICE OF INTENTION TO ENTER LAND OR PREMISES

To: [*INSERT NAME*]

1. This notice is served under section 8 of the Party Wall etc. Act 1996 ("the Act").

2. You are the owner or occupier of [*INSERT ADDRESS*] ("the Premises").

3. **I GIVE NOTICE** that I intend to enter the Premises on [*INSERT DATE*]

4. **TAKE NOTICE** that if you refuse to permit access and/or hinder or obstruct me you may be guilty of a criminal offence under section 16 of the Act.

Signed:-

.... Dated:

[*INSERT NAME*]

Precedent 10A

Party Wall etc. Act 1996, section 10(3)

NOTICE REQUESTING AGREED SURVEYOR TO ACT EFFECTIVELY

To: [*INSERT NAME*]

1. This request is served under section 10(3) of the Party Wall etc. Act 1996 ("the Act").

2. **I REQUEST** that you act effectively as follows:-

    a. [*LIST THE ACTIONS REQUIRED TO BE TAKEN*]

3. If you neglect to undertake the above actions within the period of ten days beginning on the date on which this request is served then the proceedings for settling any disputes shall recommence from the beginning.

Signed:-

.... Dated:

[*INSERT NAME*]

Precedent 10B

Party Wall etc. Act 1996, section 10(4)

REQUEST TO APPOINT A SURVEYOR

To: [*INSERT NAME*]

1. This request is made under section 10(4) of the Party Wall etc. Act 1996 ("the Act").

2. I am the owner of [*INSERT ADDRESS*]. You are the owner of [*INSERT ADDRESS*]. A dispute has arisen between us relating to the building works at [*INSERT ADDRESS*].

3. **I REQUEST** that you appoint a surveyor under section 10(1) of the Act. If you do not appoint a surveyor in writing within 10 days of service of this request on you then I will appoint a surveyor on your behalf.

Signed:-

.... Dated:

[*INSERT NAME*]

Precedent 10C

Party Wall etc. Act 1996, section 10(7)

NOTICE REQUESTING APPOINTED SURVEYOR TO ACT EFFECTIVELY

To: [*INSERT NAME*]

2. This request is served under section 10(7) of the Party Wall etc. Act 1996 ("the Act").

3. **I REQUEST** that you act effectively as follows:-

    a. [*LIST THE ACTIONS REQUIRED TO BE TAKEN*]

4. If you neglect to undertake the above actions within the period of ten days beginning on the date on which this request is served then I may proceed *ex parte* in respect of those matters and anything done by me shall be as effectual as if I had acted as an agreed surveyor.

Signed:-

.... Dated:
[INSERT NAME]

Precedent 10D

<u>Party Wall etc. Act 1996, section 10(8)</u>

REQUEST TO SELECT THIRD SURVEYOR

To: [*INSERT NAME*]

1. This request is made under section 10(8) of the Party Wall etc. Act 1996 ("the Act").

2. **I REQUEST** that you select a third surveyor within 10 days of service of this request.

3. I propose the following surveyors:-

    a. [INSERT NAMES AND ADDRESSES OF PROPOSED THIRD SURVEYORS]

4. If you do not select a third surveyor within 10 days of service of this request I shall request that a third surveyor is selected by the Appointing Officer.

Signed:-

.... Dated:
[*INSERT NAME*]

Precedent 10E

Party Wall etc. Act 1996, section 10(9)

NOTICE REQUESTING THIRD SURVEYOR TO ACT EFFECTIVELY

To: [*INSERT NAME*]

1. This request is served under section 10(9) of the Party Wall etc. Act 1996 ("the Act").

2. On [INSERT DATE] the following dispute(s) were referred to you as third surveyor:

    a. [INSERT PARTICULARS OF THE DISPUTES(S) REFERRED]

3. **I HEREBY REQUEST** that you act effectively as follows:-

    a. [*LIST THE ACTIONS REQUIRED TO BE TAKEN*]

4. If you neglect to undertake the above actions within the period of ten days beginning on the date on which this request is served then the other two surveyors will forthwith select another surveyor in your place.

Signed:-

.... Dated:

[INSERT NAME]

Precedent 11A

<u>Party Wall etc. Act 1996, section 11(10)</u>

ACCOUNT FOR INCREASED COSTS ARISING FROM SPECIAL FOUNDATIONS

1. On [INSERT DATE] a notice under the Party Wall etc. Act 1996 ("The Act") was served in respect of works at [INSERT ADDRESS] which included special foundations within the meaning of section 20 of the Party wall etc. Act 1996.

2. Written consent to those special foundations was given on [INSERT DATE].

3. The cost of erecting buildings and/or structures on [INSERT ADRESS] has been increased by £[INSERT AMOUNT] by reason of the Special Foundations.

4. The works in respect of which additional costs are claimed were completed on [INSERT DATE]

5. I require you to pay to me the sum of £[INSERT AMOUNT] as set out in the attached schedule, invoices and supporting documents upon service of this account.

Signed:-

.... Dated:

[INSERT NAME]

Precedent 12A

Party Wall etc. Act 1996, section 12(1)

NOTICE BY ADJOINING OWNER REQUESTING SECURITY FOR EXPENSES

To: [*INSERT NAME*]

1. This notice is given under section 12(1) of the Party Wall etc. Act 1996 ("the Act").

2. On [*INSERT DATE*] you served a notice under the Act relating to works at [*INSERT ADDRESS*].

3. **I HEREBY GIVE NOTICE** that I require you to give security for expenses in the sum of £[*INSERT AMOUNT*]

Signed:-

.... Dated:

[INSERT NAME]

Precedent 12B

Party Wall etc. Act 1996, section 12(2)

NOTICE BY BUILDING OWNER
REQUESTING SECURITY FOR EXPENSES

To: [*INSERT NAME*]

1. This notice is given under section 12(2) of the Party Wall etc. Act 1996 ("the Act").

2. On [*INSERT DATE*] you served a [*counter-notice under section 4*] **OR** [*a notice requesting security under section 12(1)]* of the Act relating to works at [*INSERT ADDRESS*].

3. **I HEREBY GIVE NOTICE** that I require you to give security for expenses in the sum of £[*INSERT AMOUNT*]

4. If you do not comply with this notice or dispute my request for security of expenses within one month of the date on which it was served then your [*counter-notice under section 4*] **OR** [*a notice requesting security under section 12(1)]* will cease to have effect.

Signed:-

.... Dated:
[INSERT NAME]

Precedent 13A

Party Wall etc. Act 1996, section 13(1)

BUILDING OWNER'S ACCOUNT FOR WORKS PAYABLE BY ADJONING OWNER

1. On [INSERT DATE] I completed works which you are liable to pay for under section 11 of the Party Wall etc. Act 1996 ("the Act").

2. The particulars and costs of those works including any deduction are set out in the attached schedule.

3. You may serve upon me any objection(s) you may have to this account or the attached schedule.

4. If you do not serve any objection(s) within one month of the day on which this account is served on you then you will be deemed to have no objection to the account.

Signed:-

.... Dated:

[INSERT NAME]

Precedent 17A

<u>Law of Property Act 1925, section 136</u>

DEED OF ASSIGMENT OF PARTY WALL DEBT

THIS DEED is made on [*INSERT DATE*]

1. [*INSERT NAME*] of [*INSERT ADDRESS*] ("the Owner") and

2. [*INSERT NAME*] of [*INSERT ADDRESS*] ("the Surveyor")

WHEREAS

A. An Award under the Party Wall etc. Act 1996 dated [*INSERT DATE*] provided for the sum of £[*INSERT AMOUNT*] ("the Debt") to be paid to the Owner.

B. The Owner has agreed to assign the Debt to the Surveyor

NOW THIS DEED WITNESSES as follows:

The Owner assigns the Debt to the Surveyor with full title guarantee together with all interest due and to become due upon the Debt and the full benefit and advantage of the Debt **TO HOLD** to the Surveyor absolutely.

Signed as a Deed }
by the Owner }
In the presence of } ....

Signature: ....
Name: ....
Address: ....
....
....
Occupation: ....

Precedent 17B

Law of Property Act 1925, section 136

NOTICE OF ASSIGNMENT

To: [*INSERT NAME*] of [*INSERT ADDRRESS*]

From: [*INSERT NAME*] of [*INSERT ADDRESS*]

I **HEREBY GIVE YOU NOTICE** that the sum of £[*INSERT AMOUNT*] due under the award dated [*INSERT DATE OF AWARD*] has been assigned to me.

Signed:-

.... Dated:

[INSERT NAME]

Precedent 17C

Magistrates Court Act 1980 s. 58

COMPLAINT FOR A CIVIL DEBT

Date: [*INSERT DATE*]

Defendant: [*INSERT NAME*]

Address: [*INSERT ADDRESS*]

Matter of Complaint: [*INSERT NAME*], who is the Complainant, states that an award under the Party Wall etc. Act 1996 was served upon [*INSERT NAME*] of [*INSERT ADDRESS*] ("the Defendant") on [*INSERT DATE*] which provided that the Defendant was to pay to the Complainant the sum of £[*INSERT AMOUNT*] and that the Defendant has failed to pay that sum.

THE COMPLAINANT therefore claims from the Defendant the sum of £[*INSERT AMOUNT*] due under the said award **AND** being money recoverable summarily as a civil debt

The Complaint of: [*INSERT NAME*]

Address: [*INSERT ADDRESS*]

who states that the Defendant was responsible for the matter of Complaint of which particulars are given above and claims from the Defendant the following sum which is recoverable summarily as a civil debt

Signed:-

.... Dated:

[*INSERT NAME*]

Precedent 17D

SUMMONS FOR CIVIL DEBT
Magistrates Court Act 1980 s. 51

IN THE [*INSERT NAME]*
MAGISTRATES' COURT
(Code [*INSERT COURT NUMBER*])

Date: [*INSERT DATE*]

TO THE DEFENDANT: [INSERT NAME]
Address: [INSERT ADDRESS]

YOU ARE SUMMONED to appear on:

.... at .... : ....
o'clock before the Magistrates' Court sitting at [*INSERT COURT ADDRESS*] to answer the following complaint:

Matter of Complaint: The Complainant states that an award under the Party Wall etc. Act 1996 was served upon the Defendant on [*INSERT DATE*] which provided that that the Defendant was to pay to the Complainant the sum of £[INSERT SUM].

AND that you have failed to pay the following sums which are recoverable summarily as a civil debt.

Debt: [*INSERT AMOUNT*]
Costs: [*INSERT COSTS*]

The Complainant is: [*INSERT NAME*]
Address: [*INSERT ADDRESS*]

Date of Complaint: [*INSERT DATE*]

Precedent 17E

Magistrates Court Rules 1981 r. 67

CERTIFICATE OF SERVICE OF SUMMONS

IN THE [*INSERT NAME*] MAGISTRATES' COURT
(Code [*INSERT COURT NUMBER*])

Date: [*INSERT DATE*]

I, [*INSERT NAME*] of [*INSERT ADDRESS*], **HEREBY CERTIFY** that I served the Defendant with the Summons a true copy of which is attached by [*personal service*][*First Class Post*] [*Recorded Delivery*]

Signed:-

.... Dated:
[INSERT NAME]

PART IV

EXTRACTS FROM THE

LONDON BUILDING ACTS 1774 - 1939

Party Wall etc. Act 1996		London Building Act 1939	London Building Act 1930	London Building Act 1894	Metropolitan Building Act 1855
Section 1					
(1)		45(1)	113	87	
(2)		45(1)(a)(i)	113(1)	87(1)	
(3)		45(1)(a)(ii)	113(2)	87(2)	
	(a)	45(1)(a)(ii)	113(2)	87(2)	
	(b)	45(1)(a)(ii)	113(3)	87(3)	
(4)		45(1)(a)(iii)	113(4)	87(4)	
	(a)	45(1)(a)(iii)			
	(b)	45(1)(a)(iii)	113(4)	87(4)	
(5)		45(1)(b)	113(5)	87(5)	
(6)		45(1)(c)	113(6)	87(6)	
(7)		45(1)(c)	113(6)	87(6)	
(8)			113(6)		

Party Wall etc. Act 1996		London Building Act 1939	London Building Act 1930	London Building Act 1894	Metropolitan Building Act 1855
Section 2					
(1)		46(1)			
(2)		46(1)			
	(a)	46(1)(a) & (e)	114(1) & (6)	88(1) & (6)	83(6)
	(b)	46(1)(a)	114(1) & (2)	88 (1) & (2)	83(1) & (2)
	(c)	46(1)(b)	114(3)	88(3)	83(3)
	(d)	46(1)(d)	114(5)	88(5)	83(5)
	(e)	46(1)(f)	114(7)	88(7)	83(7)

Party Wall etc. Act 1996		London Building Act 1939	London Building Act 1930	London Building Act 1894	Metropolitan Building Act 1855
	(f)	46(1)(g)	114(8)	88(8)	83(8)
	(g)	46(1)(h)	114(9)	88(9)	83(9)
	(h)	46(1)(i)	114(10)	88(10)	83(10)
	(j)				
	(k)	46(1)(j)	114(11)	88(11)	83(11)
	(l)	46(1)(k)	114(12)	88(12)	83(6)
	(m)				
	(n)				
(3)		46(1)(e)	114(6)	88(6)	
	(a)	46(1)(e)(i)	114(6)	88(6)	
	(b)	46(1)(e)(ii)	114(6)	88(6)	
(4)		46(1)(f)	114(7)	88(7)	
	(a)	46(1)(f)(i)	114(7)	88(7)	
	(b)	46(i)(f)(ii)	114(7)		
(5)		46(1)(g)(h) & (i)	114(8) - (10)	88(8) - (10)	
(6)					
(7)					
	(a)				
	(b)				
(8)		46(2)	114		

Party Wall etc. Act 1996		London Building Act 1939	London Building Act 1930	London Building Act 1894	Metropolitan Building Act 1855
Section 3					
(1)		47(1)	116(1)	90(1)	85(1)
(2)			116(1)		
	(a)	47(2)(b)	116(1)	90(1)	
	(b)	47(3)	116(4)	90(4)	85(1)
(3)		47(4)	116(1)	90(1)	
Section 4					
(1)		48(1)	115(1) & 116(5)	89(1)	84 & 85(4) - (5)
	(a)	48(2)(a)	115(1) & 116(5)	89(1) & 90(5)	84 & 85(4) - (5)
	(b)	48(2)(a)			
(2)					
	(a)	48(2)(c)	116(6)	90(6)	
	(b)	48(3)(b)	116(5)	90(5)	
(3)		48(4)	115(1)	89(1)	84
	(a)	48(4)	115(1)	89(1)	84
	(b)	48(4)	115(1)	90(4)	84
	(c)	48(4)	115(1)	89(1)	84

Party Wall etc. Act 1996		London Building Act 1939	London Building Act 1930	London Building Act 1894	Metropolitan Building Act 1855
Section 5		49	116(7)	90(7)	85(6)
Section 6					
(1)		50(1)	119	93	
	(a)	50(1)(a)	119	93	
	(b)	50(1)(a)	119	93	
(2)		50(1)			
	(a)	50(1)(b)			
	(b)	50(1)(b)			
(3)		50(1)	119	93	
(4)					
(5)		50(2)(a)	119(1)	93(1)	
(6)		50(2)(b)	119(1)	93(1)	
	(a)	50(2)(b)	119(1)	93(1)	
	(b)	50(2)(b)	119(1)	93(1)	
(7)		50(2)(c)	119(2)	93(2)	
(8)					
	(a)				
	(b)				
(9)		50(3)			
(10)		50(4)	119(4)	93(4)	

Party Wall etc. Act 1996		London Building Act 1939	London Building Act 1930	London Building Act 1894	Metropolitan Building Act 1855
Section 7					
(1)		51(1)	116(3)	90(3)	81(3)
(2)		50(2)(d)	119(3)	93(3)	
(3)		51(2)	116(2)	90(2)	
(4)		45(2) & 46(3)			
(5)		51(3)			
	(a)	51(3)(a)			
	(b)	51(b)			
Section 8					
(1)		53(1)	118	92	86
(2)		53(2)	118	92	86
(3)		53(3)	118	92	86
	(a)	53(3)(a)	118	92	86
	(b)	53(3)(b)	118	92	86
(4)		53(3)(b)	118	92	86
(5)					
(6)					
	(a)				
	(b)				

Party Wall etc. Act 1996		London Building Act 1939	London Building Act 1930	London Building Act 1894	Metropolitan Building Act 1855
Section 9					
	(a)	54	127	101	
	(b)	54	127	101	
Section 10					
(1)		55	117(1)	91(1)	85(7)
	(a)	55(a)(i)	117(1)	91(1)	85(7)
	(b)	55(a)(ii)	117(1)	91(1)	85(7)
(2)		55(h)			
(3)		55(b)	117(8)	91(8)	
	(a)	55(b)	117(8)	91(8)	
	(b)	55(b)	117(8)	91(8)	
	(c)	55(b)	117(8)	91(8)	
	(d)	55(b)	117(8)	91(8)	
(4)		55(c)	117(3)	91(3)	85(9)
	(a)	55(c)			
	(b)	55(c)	117(3)	91(3)	85(9)
(5)		55(d)	117(11)	91(11)	
(6)		55(e)		91(12)	
	(a)	55(e)		91(12)	
	(b)	55(e)		91(12)	

Party Wall etc. Act 1996		London Building Act 1939	London Building Act 1930	London Building Act 1894	Metropolitan Building Act 1855
(7)		55(e)	117 (12)	91(12)	
	(a)	55(e)	117(12)	91(12)	
	(b)	55(e)	117(12)	91(12)	
(8)		55(f)	117(10)	91(10)	
	(a)	55(f)	117(10)	91(10)	
	(b)	55(f)	117(10)	91(10)	
(9)		55(g)	117(9)	91(9)	
	(a)	55(g)	117(9)	91(9)	
	(b)	55(g)	117(9)	91(9)	
	(c)	55(g)	117(9)	91(9)	
(10)					
	(a)	55(i)			
	(b)	55(i)			
(11)					
(12)		55(k)	117(1)	91(1)	85(7)
	(a)	55(k)	117(1)	91(1)	85(7)
	(b)	55(k)	117(1)	91(1)	85(7)
	(c)	55(k)	117(1)	91(1)	85(7)
(13)		55(l)	117(4)	91(4)	85(10)
	(a)	55(l)	117(4)	91(4)	85(10)
	(b)	55(l)			

Party Wall etc. Act 1996		London Building Act 1939	London Building Act 1930	London Building Act 1894	Metropolitan Building Act 1855
	(c)				
(14)					
(15)					
	(a)				
	(b)				
(16)		55(m)	117(2)		
(17)		55(n)	117(2)	91(2)	85(8)
	(a)	55(n)(i)	117(2)	91(2)	85(8)
	(b)	55(n)(i)	117(2)	91(2)	85(8)
Section 11					
(1)		56(1)(e)	120(2)	95(2)	88(6) - (9)
(2)					
(3)		56(1)(a)			
(4)		56(1)(a) & (e)	120(2)(a)	95(1)(a)	
	(a)	56(1)(a) & (e)		95(1)(a)	
	(b)	56(1)(a) & (e)			
(5)		56(1)(a)	120(1)(a)	95(1)(b)	88(1) & (2)
	(a)	56(1)(a)	120(1)(b)	95(1(b)	88(1) & (2)
	(b)	56(1)(a)			
(6)		56(1)(e)(ii)	120(2)(b)	95(2)(b)	
(7)					

Party Wall etc. Act 1996		London Building Act 1939	London Building Act 1930	London Building Act 1894	Metropolitan Building Act 1855
	(a)				
	(b)				
(8)					
(9)		56(3)	126	100	
	(a)	56(3)	126	100	
	(b)	56(3)	126	100	
(10)		56(5)			
	(a)	56(5)			
	(b)	56(5)			
(11)		56(4)	120(3)	95(2)	
Section 12					
(1)		57(1)	121(1)	94	87
(2)		57(2)	121(2)	94	
(3)		57(3)	121(3)	94	
Section 13					
(1)		58(1)	122	96	89
(2)		58(2)	123	97	90
(3)		58(3)	124	98	91

Party Wall etc. Act 1996		London Building Act 1939	London Building Act 1930	London Building Act 1894	Metropolitan Building Act 1855
Section 14					
(1)		59(1)	126	100	93
(2)		59(2)	125	99	92
Section 15					
(1)					
	(a)				
	(b)				
	(c)				
(2)					
	(a)				
	(b)				
Section 16					
(1)					
	(a)				
	(b)				
(2)					86
	(a)				86
	(b)				86
(3)					86

Party Wall etc. Act 1996		London Building Act 1939	London Building Act 1930	London Building Act 1894	Metropolitan Building Act 1855
Section 17					
Section 18					
(1)					
(2)					
Section 19					
(1)					
	(a)				
	(b)				
	(c)				
(2)					
	(a)				
	(b)				
Section 20					
"adjoining owner"			5	5(32)	81
"appointing officer"					
"building owner"			5	5(31)	81
"foundation"		44		5(9)	
"owner"				5(29)	

Party Wall etc. Act 1996	London Building Act 1939	London Building Act 1930	London Building Act 1894	Metropolitan Building Act 1855
"party fence wall"	4(1)	5	5(18)	
"party structure"	4(1)	5	5(2)	3
"party wall"	44	5	5(16)	3
"special foundation"	44			
"surveyor"				

Section 4
London Building Act (Amendment) Act 1939

(1) In this Act save as is otherwise expressly provided therein and unless the context otherwise requires the following expressions have the meanings hereby respectively assigned to them:

"Act of 1930" means the London Building Act 1930;

"occupier" (except in Part V (Means of escape in case of fire) of this Act) does not include a lodger and the expressions "occupy" and "occupation " shall be construed accordingly;

"party fence wall" means a wall (not being part of a building) which stands on lands of different owners and is used or constructed to be used for separating such adjoining lands but does not include a wall constructed on the land of one owner the artificially formed support of which projects into the land of another owner;

"party structure" means a party wall and also a floor partition or other structure separating buildings or parts of buildings approached solely by separate staircases or separate entrances from without ;

"party wall" (except in Part VI (Rights &c. of building and adjoining owners) of this Act) means so much of a wall which forms part of a building as is used or constructed to be used for separating adjoining buildings belonging to different owners or occupied or constructed or adapted to be occupied by different persons together with the remainder (if any) of the wall vertically above such before-mentioned portion of the wall;

Section 4(2)
London Building Act (Amendment) Act 1939

(2) The definitions assigned by section 5 (Definitions) of the Act of 1930 to the following terms being terms which are defined in subsection (1) of this section namely "builder " "cubical extent" "district surveyor" "domestic building" "height" "inhabited" "noxious business" "occupier" "party fence wall" "party structure" "party wall" "public building" "superintending architect" and "tribunal of appeal" and the definitions assigned by the said section 5 to the terms "base" "bressummer" "certified building" " cross wall" "fire-resisting materials" "first storey" "foundation" "girder" "high building" "pifiar" and "upper storey" shall cease to have effect except as regards anything done or begun or any proceeding instituted before the commencement of this Act.

Section 44

London Building Act (Amendment) Act 1939

In this Part of this Act unless the context otherwise requires the following expressions have the meanings hereby respectively assigned to them :—

“foundation” in relation to a wall means the solid ground or artificially formed support resting on solid ground on which the wall rests;

"party wall" means—

(i) a wall which forms part of a building and stands on lands of different owners to a greater extent than the projection of any artificially formed support on which the wall rests; and

(ii) so much of a wall not being a wall referred to in the foregoing paragraph (i) as separates buildings belonging to different owners;

"special foundations" means foundations in which an assemblage of steel beams or rods is employed for the purpose of distributing any load.

Section 45
London Building Act (Amendment) Act 1939

(1) Where lands of different owners adjoin and are not built on at the line of junction or are built on at the line of junction only to the extent of a boundary wall (not being a party fence wall the external wall not built on and either owner is about to build on any part of the line of junction the following provisions shall have effect:

(a) If the building owner desires to build on the line of junction a party wall or party fence wall:

(i) the building owner shall serve notice of his desire on the adjoining owner describing the intended wall;

(ii) if the adjoining owner consents in writing to the building of party wall or party fence wall the wall shall be built half on the land of each of the two owners or in such other position as may be agreed between the two owners and the expense of building the wall shall be from time to time defrayed by the two owners in due proportion regard being had to the use made or to be made of the wall by the two owners respectively and to the cost of labour and materials prevailing at the time when that use is made by each owner respectively;

(iii) if the adjoining owner does not consent in writing to the building of a party wall or party fence wall the building owner shall not build the wall otherwise than at his own expense and as an external wall or a fence wall as the case may be placed wholly on his own land;

(b) If the building owner desires to build on the line of junction a wall placed wholly on his own land he shall serve notice of his desire on the adjoining owner describing the intended wall;

(c) Where in either of the cases described in paragraphs (a) and (b) of this subsection the building owner builds a wall on his own land he shall have a right at his own expense at any time after the expiration of one month but not exceeding six months from the service of the notice to place on land of the adjoining owner below the level of such land any projecting footings and foundation making compensation to the adjoining owner or the adjoining occupier or both of them for any damage occasioned thereby the amount of the compensation in the event of difference to be determined in the manner provided in this Part of this act.

(2) Nothing in this section shall authorise the building owner to place special foundations on land of the adjoining owner without his previous consent in writing.

Section 46

London Building Act (Amendment) Act 1939

(1) Where lands of different owners adjoin and at the line of junction the said lands are built on or a boundary wall being a party fence wall or the lands where junction external wall of a building has been erected the building owner shall have the following rights:

(a) A right to make good underpin thicken or repair or demolish and rebuild a party structure or party fence wall in any case where such work is necessary on account of defect or want of repair of the party structure or party fence wall;

(b) A right to demolish a timber or other partition which separates buildings belonging to different owners but is not in conformity with the London Building Acts or any byelaws made in pursuance of those Acts and to build instead a party wall in conformity therewith;

(c) A right in relation to a building having rooms or storeys belonging to different owners intermixed to demolish such of those rooms or storeys or any part thereof as are not in conformity with the London Building Acts or any byelaws made in pursuance of those Acts and to rebuild them in conformity therewith;

(d) A right (where buildings are connected by arches or structures over public ways or over passages belonging to other persons) to demolish such of those buildings arches or structures or such parts thereof as are not in conformity with the London Building Acts or any byelaws made in pursuance of those Acts and to rebuild them in conformity therewith;

(e) A right to underpin thicken or raise any party structure or party fence wall permitted by this Act to be underpinned thickened or raised or any external wall built against such a party structure or party fence wall subject to

(i) making good all damage occasioned thereby to the adjoining premises or to the internal finishings and decorations thereof; and

(ii) carrying up to such height and in such materials as may be agreed between the building owner and the adjoining owner or in the event of difference determined in the manner provided in this Part of this Act all flues and chimney stacks belonging to the adjoining owner on or against the party structure or external wall;

(f) A right to demolish a party structure which is of insufficient strength or height for the purposes of any intended building of the building owner and to rebuild it of sufficient strength or height for the said purposes subject to:

(i) making good all damage occasioned thereby to the adjoining premises or to the internal, finishings and decorations thereof; and

(ii) carrying up to such height and in such materials as may be agreed between the building owner and the adjoining owner or in the event of difference determined in the manner provided in this Part of this Act all flues and chimney stacks belonging to the adjoining owner on or against the party structure or external wall;

(g) A right to cut into a party structure subject to making good all damage occasioned thereby to the adjoining premises or to the internal finishings and decorations thereof;

(h) A right to cut away any footing or any projecting chimney breast jamb or flue or other projection on or over the land of the building owner from a party wall party fence wall external wall or boundary wall in order to erect raise or underpin an external wall against such party wall party fence wall external wall or boundary wall or for any other purpose subject to making good all damage occasioned thereby to the adjoining premises or to the internal finishings and decorations thereof;

(i) A right to cut away or demolish such parts of any wall or building of an adjoining owner overhanging the land of the building owner as may be necessary to enable a vertical wall to be erected against that wall or building subject to making good any damage occasioned thereby to the wall or building or to the internal finishings and decorations of the adjoining premises;

(j) A right to execute any other necessary works incidental to the connection of a party structure with the premises adjoining it;

(k) A right to raise a party fence wall to raise and use as a party wall a party fence wall or to demolish a party fence wall and rebuild it as a party fence wall or as a party wall.

(2) For the purposes of this section a building or structure which was erected before the commencement of this Act shall be deemed to be in conformity with the London Building Acts and any byelaws made in pursuance of those Acts if it is in conformity with the Acts and any byelaws made in pursuance of the Acts which regulated buildings or structures in London at the date at which it was erected.

Section 46(3)
London Building Act (Amendment) Act 1939

(3) Nothing in this section shall authorise the building Owner to place special foundations on land of the adjoining owner without his previous consent in writing.

Section 47
London Building Act (Amendment) Act 1939

(1) Before exercising any right conferred on structure him by section 46 (Rights of owners of adjoining lands where junction line built on) of this Act a building owner shall serve on the adjoining owner notice in writing (in this Act referred to as a "party structure notice") stating the nature and particulars of the proposed work the time at which it will be begun and those particulars shall where the building owner proposes to construct special foundations include plans sections and details of construction of the special foundations with reasonable particulars of the loads to be carried thereby.

(2) A party structure notice shall be served—

(a) in respect of a party fence wall or special foundations at least one month; and

(b) in respect of a party structure at least two months;

before the date stated therein as that on which the work is to be begun.

(3) A party structure notice shall not be effective unless the work to which the notice relates is begun within six months after the notice has been served and is prosecuted with due diligence.

(4) Nothing in this section shall prevent a building owner from exercising with the consent in writing of the adjoining owner and of the adjoining occupiers any right conferred on him by section 46 (Rights of owners of adjoining lands where junction line built on) of this Act and nothing in this section shall require him to serve any party structure notice before complying with any notice served under the provisions of Part VII (Dangerous and neglected structures) of this Act.

(1) After the service of a party structure notice the adjoining owner may serve on the building owner a notice in writing (in this Part of this Act referred to as "a counter notice ").

(2) A counter notice—

(a) may in respect of a party fence wall .or party structure require the building owner to build in or on the party fence wall or party structure as the case may be to which the notice relates such chimney copings breasts jambs or flues or such piers or recesses or other like works as may reasonably be required for the convenience of the adjoining owner;

(b) may in respect of special foundations to which the adjoining owner consents under subsection (3) of section 46 (Rights of owners of adjoining lands where junction line built on) of this Act require them to be placed at a specified greater depth than that proposed by the building owner or to be constructed of sufficient strength to bear the load to be carried by columns of any intended building of the adjoining owner or may include both of these requirements; and

(c) shall specify the works required by the notice to be executed and shall be accompanied by plans sections and particulars thereof.

(3) A counter notice shall be served—

(a) in relation to special foundations within twenty-one days after the service of the party structure notice; and

(b) in relation to any other matter within one month after the service of the party structure notice.

Section 48(4)

London Building Act (Amendment) Act 1939

(4) A building owner on whom a counter notice has been served shall comply with the requirements of the counter notice unless the execution of the works required by the counter notice would be injurious to him or cause unnecessary inconvenience to him or unnecessary delay in the execution of the works pursuant to the party structure notice.

Section 49

London Building Act (Amendment) Act 1939

If an owner on whom a party structure notice from or a counter notice has been served does not within notices, fourteen days thereafter express his consent thereto in writing he shall be deemed to have dissented from the notice and a difference shall be deemed to have arisen between the parties.

Section 50
London Building Act (Amendment) Act 1939

(1) Where a building owner:

(a) proposes to erect within ten feet from any part of a building of an adjoining owner a building or structure independent of the building of the adjoining owner and any part of the proposed building or structure will within the said ten feet extend to a lower level than the level of the bottom of the foundations of the building of the adjoining owner; or

(b) proposes to erect within twenty feet from any part of an independent building of an adjoining owner a building or structure any part of which will within the said twenty feet meet a plane drawn downwards in the direction of the building or structure of the building owner at an angle of forty-five degrees to the horizontal from the line formed by the intersection of the plane of the level of the bottom of the foundations of the building of the adjoining owner with the plane of the external face of the external wall of the building of the adjoining owner;

he may and if required by the adjoining owner shall subject to the provisions of this section at the expense of the building owner underpin or otherwise strengthen or safeguard the foundations of the building of the adjoining owner so far as may be necessary.

(2) In any case to which subsection (1) of this section applies the following provisions shall have effect :—

(a) At least one month before beginning to erect a building or structure the building owner shall serve on the adjoining owner notice in writing of his intention so to do and that notice shall state whether he proposes to underpin or otherwise strengthen or safeguard the foundations of the building of the adjoining owner;

(b) The said notice shall be accompanied by plans and sections showing the site of the building or structure proposed to be erected by the building owner and the depth to which he proposes to excavate;

(c) Within fourteen days after service of the said notice the adjoining owner may serve notice in writing on the building owner that he disputes the necessity of or requires as the case may be the underpinning or strengthening or the safeguarding of the foundations of his building and if the adjoining owner serves such a notice a difference shall be deemed to have arisen between the building owner and the adjoining owner;

(d) The building owner shall compensate the adjoining owner and any adjoining occupier for any inconvenience loss or damage which may result to any of them by reason of any work executed in pursuance of this section.

(3) On completion of any work executed in pursuance of this section the building owner shall if so requested by the adjoining owner supply him with particulars including plans and sections of the work.

(4) Nothing in this section shall relieve the building owner from any liability to which he would otherwise be subject for injury to the adjoining owner or any adjoining occupier by reason of work executed by him.

Section 51

London Building Act (Amendment) Act 1939

(1) A building owner shall not exercise any right conferred on him by this Part of this Act in such manner or at such time as to cause unnecessary inconvenience to the adjoining owner or to the adjoining occupier.

(2) Where a building owner in exercising any right conferred on him by this Part of this Act lays open any part of the adjoining land or building he shall at his own expense make and maintain so long as may be necessary a proper hoarding shoring or fans or temporary construction for the protection of the adjoining land or building and the security of the adjoining occupier.

(3) Any works executed in pursuance of this Part of this Act shall—

(a) comply with the provisions of the London Building Acts and any byelaws made in pursuance of those Acts; and

(b) subject to the foregoing paragraph (a) be executed in accordance with such plans sections and particulars as may be agreed between the owners or in the event of difference determined in the manner provided in this Part of this Act and no deviation shall be made therefrom except such as may also be agreed between the parties or in the event of difference determined in manner aforesaid.

Section 52

London Building Act (Amendment) Act 1939

Where a building owner proposes to erect any building or structure or carry out any work in relation to a building or structure on land which abuts on a street or way less than twenty feet in width the following provisions shall have effect if the erection of the proposed building or structure or the carrying out of the work involves excavation to a depth of twenty feet or more below the level of the highest part of the land immediately abutting on the street:

(a) Notices stating the place (being a place situate at a distance not greater than two miles of such land) at and the hours during which plans and sections of so much of the proposed building structure or work as relates to the excavation may be inspected shall be exhibited in a prominent position on the land or on any existing building on the boundary wall fence or hoarding (if any) surrounding the said land or building and in such a manner as to be readily legible from every street or way on which the land abuts;

(b) The notices shall be exhibited at least four weeks before any such work of excavation is begun and shall be maintained and where necessary renewed by the building owner until such work of excavation is begun;

(c) The plans and sections referred to in the notices shall until the work of excavation is begun be open to public inspection without payment at the place and during such reasonable hours as are stated in the notice.

Section 53
London Building Act (Amendment) Act 1939

(1) A building owner his servants agents and workmen may during usual working hours enter and remain on any premises for the purpose of executing and may execute any work in pursuance of this Part of this Act and may remove any furniture or fittings or take any other action necessary for that purpose.

(2) If the premises are closed the building owner his servants agents and workmen may if accompanied by a constable or other police officer break open any fences or doors in order to enter the premises.

(3) Before entering any premises in pursuance of this section a building owner shall give to the owner and occupier of the premises—

(a) in case of emergency such notice of his intention to enter as may be reasonably practicable;

(b) in any other case fourteen days' notice of his intention to enter

Section 54

London Building Act (Amendment) Act 1939

Nothing in this Part of this Act shall authorise any interference with any easement of light or other easement in or relating to a party wall or prejudicially affect the right of any person to preserve any right in connection with a party wall which is demolished or rebuilt and to take any necessary steps for that purpose.

Section 55
London Building Act (Amendment) Act 1939

Where a difference arises or is deemed to have arisen between a building owner and an adjoining owner in respect of any matter connected with any work to which this Part of this Act relates the following provisions shall have effect:

(a) Either:

  (i) both parties shall concur in the appointment of one surveyor (in this section referred to as an "agreed surveyor"); or

  (ii) each party shall appoint a surveyor and the two surveyors so appointed shall select a third surveyor (all of whom are in this section together referred to as "the three surveyors");

(b) If an agreed surveyor refuses or for ten days after a written request by either party neglects to act or if before the difference is settled lie dies or becomes incapable of acting the proceedings for settling such difference shall begin de novo;

(c) If either party to the difference refuses or for ten days after a written request by the other party neglects to appoint a surveyor under subparagraph (ii) of paragraph (a) of this section that other party may make the appointment on his behalf;

(d) If before the difference is settled a surveyor appointed under subparagraph (ii) of paragraph (a) of this section by a party to the difference dies or becomes incapable of acting the party appointed him may appoint another surveyor in his place who shall have the same power and authority as his predecessor;

(e) If a surveyor appointed wider subparagraph (ii) of paragraph (a) of this section by a party to the difference or if a surveyor appointed wider paragraph (d) of this section refuses or for ten days after a written request by either party neglects to act the surveyor of the other party may proceed ex parte and anything so done by him shall be as effectual as if he had been an agreed surveyor;

(f) If a surveyor appointed under subparagraph (ii) of paragraph (a) of this section by a party to the difference refuses or for ten days after a written request by either party neglects to select a third surveyor under paragraph (a) or paragraph (g) of this section the superintending architect or in cases where the Council is a party to the difference the Secretary of State may on the application of either party select a third surveyor shall have the same power and authority as if he had been selected under paragraph (a) or paragraph (g) of this section;

(g) If a third surveyor selected under subparagraph (ii) of paragraph (a) of this section refuses or for ten days after a written request by either party or the surveyor appointed by either party neglects to act or if before the difference is settled he dies or becomes incapable of acting the other two of the three surveyors, shall forthwith select another surveyor in his place who shall have the same power and authority as his predecessor;

(h) All appointments and selections made under this section shall be in writing;

(i) The agreed surveyor or as the case may be the three surveyors or any two of them shall settle by award any matter which before the commencement of any work to which a notice under this Part of this Act relates or from time to time during the continuance of such work

Section 55(h)(i)

London Building Act (Amendment) Act 1939
Continued

may be in dispute between the building owner and the adjoining owner;

(j) If no two of the three surveyors are in agreement the third surveyor selected in pursuance of this section shall make the award within fourteen days after he is called upon to do so;

(k) The award may determine the right to execute and the time and manner of executing any work and generally any other matter arising out of or incidental to the difference:

Provided that any period appointed by the award for executing any work shall not unless otherwise agreed between the building owner and the adjoining owner begin to run until after the expiration of the period prescribed by this Act for service of the notice in respect of which the difference arises or is deemed to have arisen;

(l) The costs incurred in making or obtaining an award under this section and the cost of reasonable supervision of carrying out any work to which the award relates shall subject to the provisions of this section be paid by such of the parties as the surveyor or surveyors making the award determine;

(m) The award shall be conclusive and shall not except as provided by this section be questioned in any court;

(n) Either of the parties to the difference may within fourteen days after the delivery of an award made under this section appeal to the county court against the award and the following provisions shall have effect:

(i) Subject as hereafter in this paragraph provided the county court may rescind the award or modify it in such manner and make such order as to costs as it thinks fit;

(ii) If the appellant against the award on appearing before the county court is unwilling that the matter should be decided by that court and satisfies that court that he will if the matter is decided against him be liable to pay a sum (exclusive of costs) exceeding one hundred pounds and gives security approved by the county court to prosecute his appeal in the High Court and to abide the event thereof all proceedings in the county court shall be stayed and the appellant may bring an action in the High Court against the other party to the difference;

(o) Where an appellant against an award brings an action in the High Court in pursuance of the last preceding paragraph the following provisions shall have effect :

(i) If the parties agree as to the facts a special case may be stated for the opinion of the court and may be dealt with in accordance with or as nearly as circumstances admit in accordance with the rules of the court;

(ii) In any other case the plaintiff in the action shall deliver to the defendant an issue whereby the matters in difference may be tried;

(iii) The issue shall be in such form as may be agreed between the parties or in case of dispute or of non-appearance of the defendant as may be settled by the court;

Section 55(n)(i)
London Building Act (Amendment) Act 1939
Continued

(vi) The action shall proceed and the issue be tried in accordance with or as nearly as circumstances admit in accordance with the rules of the court;

(v) Any costs incurred by the parties in the county court shall be deemed to be costs incurred in the action in the High Court and be payable accordingly.

Section 56

London Building Act (Amendment) Act 1939

(1) The following provisions shall apply with respect to the apportionment of expenses as between respect of the building owner and the adjoining owner:

(a) Expenses incurred in the exercise of the rights conferred by paragraph (a) of subsection (1) of section 46 (Rights of owners of adjoining lands where junction line built on) of this Act shall be defrayed by the building owner and the adjoining owner in due proportion regard being had to the use which the two owners respectively make or may make of the party structure or party fence wall;

(b) Expenses incurred in the exercise of the rights conferred by paragraph (b) of subsection (1) of the said section together with the expenses of building any additional party structure that may be required by reason of the exercise of those rights shall be defrayed by the building owner and the adjoining owner in due proportion regard being had to the use which the two owners respectively make or may make of the party wall or party structure and the thickness of such party wall or party structure required for support of the respective buildings of the two owners;

(c) Expenses incurred in the exercise of the rights conferred by paragraph (c) of subsection (1) of the said section shall be defrayed by the building owner and the adjoining owner in due proportion regard being had to the use which the two owners respectively make or may make of the rooms or storeys rebuilt;

(d) Expenses incurred in the exercise of the rights conferred by paragraph (d) of subsection (1) of the said section shall be defrayed by the building owner and the adjoining owner in due proportion regard being had to the use which the two owners respectively make or may make of the buildings arches or structures rebuilt;

(e) Expenses incurred in the exercise of the rights conferred by—

(i) paragraphs (e) (g) (1&) (i) and (k) of subsection (1) of the said section;

(ii) paragraph (f) of subsection (I) of the said section in so far as the expenses are not expenses inourre4 in the exercise of any rights conferred by other paragraphs of the said subsection and also a fair allowance in respect of the disturbance and inconvenience caused where the expenses have been incurred in the exercise of the rights conferred by the said paragraph (f);

shall be defrayed by the building owner,

(2) Expenses incurred in the exercise of the rights conferred by paragraph (j) of subsection (1) of the said section shall be defrayed in the same manner as the expenses of the work to which they are incidental.

(3) Any expenses reasonably incurred by the building owner in executing any works in pursuance of a counter notice served on him by an adjoining owner under section 48 notices) of this Act shall be defrayed by the adjoining owner.

(4) If at any time during the execution or after the completion of works carried out in the exorcise of the rights conferred by paragraphs (e) (f) (5) or (k) of section (1) of section 46 (Rights of owners of adjoining lands where junction line built on) of this Act any use of those works or any part thereof is made by the adjoining owner additional to the use thereof made by him at the

time when the works began a due proportion of the expenses incurred by the building owner in the exercise of the rights conferred by any of the said paragraphs regard being had to the additional use of the works made by the adjoining owner shall be defrayed by the adjoining owner.

(5) Where in pursuance of section 45 (Rights of owners of adjoining lands where junction line not built on) or the said section 46 of this consent in writing has been given to the construction of special foundations on 'land of an adjoining owner, then if the adjoining owner erects any building or structure and its cost is found to be increased by reason of the existence of the said foundations the owner of the building to which the said foundations belong shall on receiving. an account with any necessary vouchers within two months after the completion of the work by the adjoining owner repay to the adjoining owner so much of the cost as due to the existence of the said foundations.

(6) Where under this Section expenses are to be defrayed in due proportion regard being had to the use made by an owner of a party structure party fence wall external wall or other work regard shall unless otherwise agreed between the building owner and the adjoining owner or provided in the award also be had to the cost of labour and materials prevailing at the time when that use is made.

Section 57
London Building Act (Amendment) Act 1939

(1) An adjoining owner may by notice in writing require the building owner before he begins any work in the exercise of the rights conferred by this Part of this Act to give such security as may be agreed between the owners or in the event of dispute determined by a judge of the county court for the payment of all such expenses costs and compensation in respect of the work as may be payable by the building owner.

(2) Where in the exercise of the rights conferred by this Part of this Act an adjoining owner requires a building owner to carry out any work the expenses of which are to be defrayed in whole or in part by the adjoining owner or where the adjoining owner serves a notice on the building owner under subsection (1) of this section the building owner may before beginning the work to which the requirement or notice relates serve a notice in writing on the adjoining owner requiring him to give such security as may be agreed between the owners or in the event of dispute determined by a judge of the county court for the payment of such expenses costs and compensation in respect of the work as may be payable by him.

(3) If within one month after receiving a notice under subsection (2) of this section or in the event of dispute after the date of the determination by the judge of the county court the adjoining owner does not comply therewith the requirement or notice by him to which the building owner's notice under that subsection relates shall cease to have effect.

Section 58
London Building Act (Amendment) Act 1939

(1) Within two months after the completion expenses. of any work executed by a building owner of which the expenses are to be wholly or partially defrayed by an adjoining owner in accordance with section 56 (Expenses in respect of party structures) of this Act the building owner shall deliver to the adjoining owner an account in showing:

(a) particulars and expenses of the work; and

(b) any deductions to which the adjoining owner or any other person is entitled in respect of old materials or otherwise;

and in preparing the account the work shall be estimated and valued at fair average rates and prices according to the nature of the work the locality and the cost of labour and materials prevailing at the time when the work is executed.

(2) Within one month after delivery of the said account the adjoining owner may give notice in writing to the building owner stating any objection he may have thereto and thereupon a difference shall be deemed to have arisen between the parties.

(3) If within the said month the adjoining owner does not give notice under subsection (2) of this section he shall be deemed to have no objection to the account.

Section 59

London Building Act (Amendment) Act 1939

(1) All expenses to be defrayed by an adjoining owner in accordance with an account delivered under section 58 (Account of expenses) of this Act shall be paid by the adjoining owner and in default may be recovered as a debt.

(2) Until an adjoining owner pays to the building owner such expenses as aforesaid the property in any works executed under this Part of this Act to which the expenses relate shall be vested solely in the building owner.

Section 5
London Building Act 1930

In this Act save as is otherwise expressly provide therein and unless the context otherwise requires the following expressions have the meanings hereby respectively assigned to them (that is to say) :—

"adjoining owner" and "adjoining occupier" respectively mean any owner and any occupier of land buildings storeys or rooms adjoining those of the building owner;

“builder" means the person who is employed to build or to execute work on a building or structure or where no person is so employed the owner of the building or structure;

"building owner" means such one of the owners of adjoining land as is desirous of building or such one of the owners of buildings storeys or rooms separated from one another by a party wall or party structure as does or is desirous of doing a work affecting that party wall or party structure:

"external wall" means an outer wall or vertical enclosure of any building not being a party wall;

"occupier" does not include a lodger and the expressions "occupy" and "occupation" shall be construed accordingly;

"owner" includes every person in possession or receipt either of the whole or of any part of the rents or profits of any land or tenement or in the occupation of any land or tenement otherwise than as a tenant from year to year or for any less term or as a tenant at will;

"party arch" means an arch separating adjoining buildings storeys or rooms belonging to different owners or occupied or constructed or adapted to be occupied by different persons or separating a building from a public way or a private way leading to premises in other occupation;

Section 5
London Building Act 1930
Continued

"party fence wall "means a wall used or constructed to be used as a separation of adjoining lands of different owners and standing on lands of different owners and not being part of a building but does not include a wall constructed on the land of one owner the footings of which project into the land of another owner;

"party structure" means a party wall and a partition floor or other structure separating vertically or horizontally buildings storeys or rooms approached by distinct staircases or separate entrances from without;

"party wall" means-

(a) a wall forming part of a building used or constructed to be used for separation of adjoining buildings belonging to different owners or occupied or constructed or adapted to be occupied by different persons; or

(b) a wall forming part of a building and standing to a greater extent than the projection of the footings on lands of different owners;

Section 113
London Building Act 1930

Where lands of different owners adjoin and are owners of unbuilt on at the line of junction and either owner is about to build on any part of the line of junction the following provisions shall have effect

(1) If the building owner desires to build a party wall on the line of junction he may serve notice thereof on the adjoining owner describing the intended wall:

(2) If the adjoining owner consents to the building of a party wall the wall shall be built half on the land of each of the two owners or in such other position as may be agreed between the two owners:

(3) The expense of the building of the party wall shall be from time to time defrayed by the two owners in due proportion regard being had to the use made or to be made of the wall by the two owners respectively:

(4) If the adjoining owner does not consent to the building of a party wall the building owner shall not build the wall otherwise than as an external wall placed wholly on his own land:

(5) If the building owner does not desire to build a party wall on the line of junction but desires to build an external wall placed wholly on his own land he may serve notice thereof on the adjoining owner describing the intended wall:

(1) Where in either of the cases aforesaid the building owner proceeds to build an external wall on his own land he shall have a right at his own expense at any time after the expiration of one month from the service of the notice to place on the land of the adjoining owner below the level of the lowest floor the projecting footings of the external wall with concrete or other solid substructure thereunder making compensation to the adjoining

Section 113(6)
London Building Act 1930
Continued

owner or occupier for any damage occasioned thereby the amount of such compensation if any difference arises to be determined in the manner in which differences between building owners and adjoining owners are hereinafter directed to be determined.

Section 114
London Building Act 1930

The building owner shall have the following rights in relation to party structures (that is to say) :

(1) A right to make good underpin or repair any party structure which is defective or out of repair:

(2) A right to pull down and rebuild any party structure which is so far defective or out of repair as to make it necessary or desirable to pull it down:

(3) A right to pull down any timber or other partition which divides any buildings and does not conform to this Act and to build instead a party wall conforming thereto:

(4) In the case of buildings having rooms or storeys being the property of different owners intermixed a right to pull down such of the said rooms or storeys or any part thereof as are not built in conformity with this Act and to rebuild the same in conformity with this Act:

(5) In the case of buildings connected by arches or communications over public ways or over passages belonging to other persons a right to pull down such of the said buildings arches or communications or such parts thereof as are not built in conformity with this Act and to rebuild the same in conformity with this Act:

(6) A right to raise and underpin any party structure permitted by this Act to be raised or underpinned or any external wall built against such party structure upon condition of making good all damage occasioned thereby to the adjoining premises or to the internal finishings and decorations thereof and of carrying up to the requisite height all flues and chimney stacks belonging to the adjoining owner on or against such party structure or external wall:

Section 114(7)
London Building Act 1930

(7) A right to pull down any party structure which is of insufficient strength for any building intended to be built and to rebuild the same of sufficient strength for the above purpose upon condition of making good all damage occasioned thereby to the adjoining premises or to the internal finishings and decorations thereof:

(8) A right to cut into any party structure upon condition of making good all damage occasioned to the adjoining premises by such operation:

(9) A right to cut away any footing or any chimney breasts jambs or flues projecting or other projections from any party wall or external walls in order to erect an external wall against such party wall or for any other purpose upon condition of making good all damage occasioned to the adjoining premises by such operation:

(10) A right to cut away or take down such parts of any wall or building of an adjoining owner as may be necessary in consequence of such wall or building overhanging the ground of the building owner in order to erect an upright wall against the same on condition of making good any damage sustained by the wall or building by reason of such cutting away or taking down:

(11) A right to perform any other necessary works incident to the connection of a party structure with the premises adjoining thereto:

(12) A right to raise a party fence wall or to pull the same down and rebuild it as a party wall:

Section 114(12)
London Building Act 1930
Continued

Provided that all the rights conferred by paragraphs (1) to (11) inclusive of this section shall be subject to this qualification that any building which was erected previously to the first day of January eighteen hundred and ninety-five shall be deemed to comply with the provisions of this Act if it complies with the provisions of the Acts of Parliament regulating buildings in London before that date.

Section 115

London Building Act 1930

(1) Where a building owner proposes to exercise any of the foregoing rights with respect to party adjoining structures the adjoining owner may by notice require the building owner to build on any such party structure such chimney copings jambs or breasts or flues or such piers or recesses or any other like works as may fairly be required for the convenience of such adjoining owner and are specified in the notice and it shall be the duty of the building owner to comply with such requisition in all cases where the execution of the required works will not be injurious to the building owner or cause to him unnecessary inconvenience or unnecessary delay in the exercise of his right.

(2) Any difference between a building owner and an adjoining owner in respect of the execution of any such works shall be determined in the manner in which differences between building owners and adjoining owners are hereinafter directed to be determined.

Section 116

London Building Act 1930

(1) A building owner shall not except with the consent in writing of the adjoining owner and of the adjoining occupiers or in cases where any wall or party structure is dangerous (in which cases the provisions adjoining of Part X of this Act shall apply) exercise any of his rights under this Act in respect of any party fence wall unless at least one month or in respect of any party wall or party structure other than a party fence wall unless at least two months before doing so he has served on the adjoining owner a party wall or party structure notice stating the nature and particulars of the proposed work and the time at which the work is proposed to be commenced.

(2) When a building owner in the exercise of any of his rights under this Part of this Act lays open any part of the adjoining land or building he shall at his own expense make and maintain for a proper time a proper hoarding and shoring or temporary construction for protection of the adjoining land or building and the security of the adjoining occupier.

(3) A building owner shall not exercise any right by this Act given to him in such manner or at such time as to cause unnecessary inconvenience to the adjoining owner or to the adjoining occupier.

(4) A party wall or party structure notice shall not be available for the exercise of any right unless the work to which the notice relates is begun within six months after the service thereof and is prosecuted with due diligence.

(5) Within one month after receipt of such notice the adjoining owner may serve on the building owner a notice requiring him to build on any such party structure any works to the construction of which he is hereinbefore declared to be entitled.

Section 116(6)

London Building Act 1930

(6) The last-mentioned notice shall specify the works required by the adjoining owner for his convenience and shall if necessary be accompanied by explanatory plans and drawings.

(7) If either owner does not within fourteen days after the service on him of any notice under this section express his consent thereto he shall be considered as having dissented therefrom and thereupon a difference shall be deemed to have arisen between the building owner and the adjoining owner.

Section 117
London Building Act 1930

(1) In all cases not specially provided for by this Act where a difference arises between a building owner and an adjoining owner in respect of any matter connected with any work to which any notice given under this Part of this Act relates unless both parties concur in the appointment of one surveyor they shall each appoint a surveyor and the two surveyors so appointed shall select a third surveyor and such one surveyor or three surveyors or any two of them shall settle any matter from time to time during the continuance of any work to which the notice relates in dispute between such building and adjoining owner with power by his or their award to determine the right to do and the time and manner of doing any work and generally any other matter arising out of or incidental to such difference but any time so appointed for doing any work shall not unless otherwise agreed begin until after the expiration of the period by this Part of this Act prescribed for the notice in the particular case.

(2) Any award given by such one surveyor or by such three surveyors or by any two of them shall be conclusive and shall not be questioned in any court with this exception that either of the parties to the difference may appeal therefrom to the county court within fourteen days from the date of the delivery of the award and the county court may subject as hereafter :in this section provided rescind the award or modify it in such manner as it thinks just.

(3) If either party to the difference makes default in appointing a surveyor for ten days after notice has been served on him by the other party to make such appointment the party giving the notice may make the appointment in the place of the party so making default.

(4) The costs incurred in making or obtaining the award shall be paid by such party as the surveyor or surveyors determine.

Section 117(5)
London Building Act 1930

(5) If the appellant from any such award on appearing before the county court declares his unwillingness to have the matter decided by that court and proves to the satisfaction of the judge of that court that in the event of the matter being decided against him he will be liable to pay a exclusive of costs exceeding fifty pounds and gives security to be approved by the judge duly to prosecute his appeal and to abide the event thereof all proceedings in the county court shall thereupon be stayed and the appellant may bring an action in the High Court against the other party to the difference.

(6) The plaintiff in such action shall deliver to the defendants an issue whereby the matters in difference between them may be tried and the form of such issue in case of dispute or in case of the non-appearance of the defendant shall be settled by the High Court and such action shall be prosecuted and issue tried in the same manner and subject to the same incidents in and subject to which actions are prosecuted and issues tried in other cases within the jurisdiction of the High Court or as near thereto as circumstances admit.

(7) If the parties to any such action agree as to the facts a special case may be stated for the opinion of the High Court and any case so stated may be brought before the court in like manner and subject to the same incidents in and subject to which other special cases are brought before such court or as near thereto as circumstances admit and any costs incurred in the county court by the parties to such action as is mentioned in this section shall be deemed to be costs incurred in the action and be payable accordingly.

(8) Where both parties to the difference have concurred in the appointment of one surveyor for the settlement of such difference then if such surveyor refuses or for seven days neglects to act or dies or becomes incapable of acting before he has made his award the matters in dispute shall be determined

in the same manner as if such single surveyor had not been appointed.

(9) Where each party to the difference has appointed a surveyor for the settlement of the difference and a third surveyor has been selected then if such third surveyor refuses or for seven days neglects to act or before such difference is settled dies or becomes incapable of acting the two surveyors shall forthwith select another third surveyor in his place and every third surveyor so selected as last aforesaid shall have the same powers and authorities as were vested in his predecessor.

(10) Where each party to the difference has appointed a surveyor for the settlement of the difference then if the two surveyors so appointed refuse or for seven days after request of either party neglect to select a third surveyor or another third surveyor in the event of the refusal or neglect to act or death or incapacity of the third surveyor for the time being the Secretary of State may on the application of either party select some fit person to act as third surveyor and every surveyor so selected shall have the same powers and authorities as if he had been selected by the two surveyors appointed by the parties.

(11) Where each party to the difference has appointed a surveyor for the settlement of the difference then if before such difference is settled either surveyor so appointed dies or becomes incapable of acting the party by whom such surveyor was appointed may appoint in writing some other surveyor to act in his place and if for the space of seven days after notice served on him by the other party for that purpose he fails so to act the other surveyor may proceed ex parte and the decision of such other surveyor shall be as effectual as if he had been a single surveyor in whose appointment both parties had concurred and every surveyor so to be substituted as aforesaid shall have the same powers and authorities as were vested in the former surveyor at the time of his death or disability as aforesaid.

Section 117(12)
London Building Act 1930

(12) Where each party to the difference has appointed a surveyor for the settlement of the difference then if either of the surveyors refuses or for seven days neglects to act the other surveyor may proceed ex parte and the decision of such other surveyor shall be as effectual as if he had been a single surveyor in whose appointment both parties had concurred.

Section 118
London Building Act 1930

A building owner his servants agents and workmen at all usual times of working may enter and remain on any premises for the purpose of executing and may execute any work which he has become entitled or is required in pursuance of this Act to execute removing any furniture or doing any other necessary thing and if the premises are closed he and they may if accompanied by a constable or other police officer break open any fences or doors in order to effect such entry:

Provided that before entering on any premises for the purposes of this section the building owner shall except in the case of emergency give fourteen days' notice of his intention so to do to the owner and occupier and in case of emergency shall give such notice as may be reasonably practicable.

Section 119
London Building Act 1930

Where a building owner intends to erect within ten feet of a building belonging to an adjoining owner a building or structure any part of which within such ten feet extends to a lower level than the foundations of the building belonging to the adjoining owner he may and if required by the adjoining owner shall (subject as hereinafter provided) underpin or otherwise strengthen the foundations of the said building so far as may be necessary and the following provisions shall have effect:

(1) At least two months' notice in shall be given by the, building owner to the adjoining owner stating his intention to build and whether he proposes to underpin otherwise strengthen the foundations of the said building and such notice shall be accompanied by a plan and sections showing the site of the proposed building and the depth to which he proposes to excavate:

(2) If the adjoining owner within fourteen days after being served with such notice gives a counter notice in writing that he disputes the necessity of or requires such underpinning or strengthening a difference shall be deemed to have arisen between the building owner and the adjoining owner:

(3) The building owner shall be liable to compensate the adjoining owner and occupier for inconvenience loss or damage which may result to them by reason of the exercise of the powers conferred by this section:

(4) Nothing in this section shall relieve the building owner from any liability to which he would otherwise be subject in case of injury caused by his building operations to the adjoining owner.

Section 120
London Building Act 1930

(1) The following provisions shall apply with respect to expenses to be borne jointly by the building owner and adjoining owner :

(a) If any party structure is defective or out of repair the expense of making good underpinning or repairing the same shall be borne by the building owner and adjoining owner in due proportion regard being had to the use that each owner makes or may make of the structure;

(b) If any party structure is pulled down and rebuilt by reason of its being so far defective or out of repair as to make it necessary or desirable to pull it down the expense of such pulling down and rebuilding shall be borne by the building owner and adjoining owner in due proportion regard being had to the use that each owner may make of the structure;

(c) If any timber or other partition dividing a building is pulled down in exercise of the right by this Part of this Act vested in a building owner and a party structure is built instead thereof the expense of building such party structure and also of building any additional party structures that may be required by reason of the partition having been pulled down shall be borne by the building owner and adjoining owner in due proportion regard being had to the use that each owner may make of the party structure and to the thickness required for support of the respective buildings parted thereby;

(d) If any rooms or storeys or any parts thereof the property of different owners and intermixed in any building are pulled down in pursuance of the right by this Part of this Act vested in a building owner and are rebuilt in conformity with this Act the expense of such pulling down and rebuilding shall be borne by the building owner and adjoining owner in due proportion regard being had to the use that each owner may make of such rooms or storeys;

Section 120(1)(e)
London Building Act 1930

(e) If any arches or communications over public ways or over passages belonging to persons other than the owners of the buildings connected by such arches or communications or any parts thereof are pulled down in pursuance of the right by this Part of this Act vested in a building owner and are rebuilt in conformity with this Act the expense of such pulling down and rebuilding shall be borne by the building owner and adjoining owner in due proportion regard being had to the use that each owner may make of such arches or communications.

(2) The following provisions shall apply with respect to expenses to be borne by the building owner:

(a) If any party structure or any external wall built against another external wall is raised or underpinned in pursuance of the power by this Part of this Act vested in a building owner the expense of raising or underpinning the same and of making good all damage occasioned thereby and of carrying up to the requisite height all such flues and chimney-stacks belonging to the adjoining owner on or against Any such party structure or external wall as are by this Part of this Act required to be made good and carried up shall be borne by the building owner;

(b) If any party structure which is of proper materials and sound or not so far defective or out of repair as to make it necessary or desirable to pull it down is pulled down and rebuilt by the building owner the expense of pulling down and rebuilding the same and of making good any damage by this Part of this Act required to be made good and a fair allowance in respect of the disturbance and inconvenience caused to the adjoining owner shall be borne by the building owner;

(c) If any party structure is cut into by the building owner the expense of cutting into the same and of making good any damage by this Part of this Act required to be made good shall be borne by such building owner;

(d) If any footing chimney breast jamb or floor is cut away in pursuance of the powers by this Part of this Act vested in a building owner the expense of such cutting away and of making good any damage by this Part of this Act required to be made good shall be borne by the building owner;

(e) If any party fence wall is raised for a building the expense of raising such wall shall be borne by the building owner;

(f) If any party fence wall is pulled down and built as a party wall the expense of pulling down such party fence wall and building the same as a party wall shall be borne by the building owner.

(3) If at any time the adjoining owner makes use of any party structure or external wall (or any part thereof) raised or underpinned as aforesaid or of any party fence wall pulled down and built as a party wall (or any part thereof) beyond the use thereof made by him before the alteration there shall be borne by the adjoining owner from time to time a due proportion of the expenses (regard being had to the use that the adjoining owner may make thereof):

(i) of raising or underpinning such party structure or external wall and of making good all such damage occasioned thereby to the adjoining owner and of carrying up to the requisite height all such flues and chimney-stacks belonging to the adjoining owner on or against any such party structure or external wall as are by this Part of this Act required to be made good and carried up; and

Section 120(2(3)(ii)
London Building Act 1930

(ii) of pulling down and building such party fence wall as a party wall.

Section 121
London Building Act 1930

(1) An adjoining owner may if he thinks fit by notice in writing require the building owner (before by beginning any work which he may be authorised by this Part of this Act to execute) to give such security as may be agreed upon or in case of difference as may be settled by the judge of the county court for the payment of all such expenses costs and compensation in respect of the work as may be payable by the building owner.

(2) The building owner may if he thinks fit at any time after service on him of a notice under the last foregoing subsection by the adjoining owner and before beginning a work to which the notice relates but not afterwards serve a counter notice on the adjoining owner requiring him to give such security for payment of the expenses costs and compensation for which he is or will be liable as may be agreed upon or in case of difference may be settled as aforesaid.

(3) If the adjoining owner does not within one month after service of such a counter notice as aforesaid give security accordingly he shall at the end of that month be deemed to have ceased to be entitled to compliance with his notice served under subsection (1) of this section and the building owner may proceed as if no such notice had been served on him by the adjoining owner.

Section 122

London Building Act 1930

Within one month after the completion of any work which a building owner is by this Part of this Act authorised or required to execute and the expense of which is in whole or in part to be borne by an adjoining owner the building owner shall deliver to the adjoining owner an account in writing of the particulars and expense of the work specifying any deduction to which such adjoining owner or other person may be entitled in respect of old materials or in other respects and every such work shall be estimated and valued at fair average rates and prices according to the nature of the work and the locality and the market price of materials and labour for the time being.

Section 123
London Building Act 1930

At any time within one month after the owner may delivery of the said account the adjoining owner if dissatisfied therewith may declare his dissatisfaction to the building owner by notice in writing served by himself or his agent and specifying his objection thereto and thereupon a difference shall be deemed to have arisen between the parties and shall be determined in manner hereinbefore in this Part of this Act provided for the settlement of differences between building and adjoining owners.

Section 124
London Building Act 1930

If within the said period of one month the does not declare in the said manner his dissatisfaction with the account he shall be deemed to have accepted the same and shall pay the same on demand to the party delivering the account and if he fails to do so the amount so due may be recovered as a debt.

Section 125
London Building Act 1930

Where the adjoining owner is liable to contribute to the expenses of building any party structure then until such contribution is paid the building owner at whose expense the same was built shall stand possessed of the sole property in the structure.

Section 126
London Building Act 1930

The adjoining owner shall be liable for all expenses incurred on his requisition by the building owner and in default the amount of those expenses may be recovered from him as a debt.

Section 127
London Building Act 1930

Nothing in this Act shall any authorise any interference with an easement of light or other easements in or relating to a party wall or prejudicially affect any right of any person to preserve or restore any light or other thing in or connected with a party wall in case of the party wall being pulled down or rebuilt.

Section 5

Metropolitan Building Act 1894

In this Act unless the context otherwise requires:

(7) The expression "bressummer" means a wooden beam or a metallic girder which carries a wall.

(9) The expression "foundation" applied to a wall having footings means the solid ground or artificially formed support on which the footings of the wall rest but in the case of a wall carried by a bressummer means such bressummer.

(15) The expression "external wall" means an outer wall or vertical enclosure of any building not being a party wall.

(16) The expression "party wall" means:

(a) A wall forming part of a building and used or constructed to be used for separation of adjoining buildings belonging to different owners or occupied or constructed or adapted to be occupied by different persons; or

(b) A wall forming part of a building and standing to a greater extent than the projection of the footings on the lands of different owners.

(18) The expression "party fence wall" means a wall used or constructed to be used as a separation of adjoining lands of different owners and standing on lands of different owners and not being part of a building but does not include a wall constructed on the land of one owner the footings of which project into the land of another owner.

(20) The expression "party structure" means a party wall and also a partition floor or other structure separating vertically or horizontally buildings storeys or rooms approached by distinct staircases or separate entrances from without.

Section 5(29)

Metropolitan Building Act 1894

(29) The expression "owner" shall apply to every person in possession or receipt either of the whole or of any part of the rents or profits of any land or tenement or in the occupation of any land or tenement otherwise than as a tenant from year to year or for any less term or as a tenant at will.

(30) The expression "occupier" does not include a lodger and "occupy" and "occupation" do not refer to occupation by a lodger.

(31) The expression “building owner” means such one of the owners of adjoining land as is desirous of building or such one of the owners of buildings storeys or rooms separated from one another by a party wall or party structure as does or is desirous of doing a work affecting that party wall or party structure.

(32) The expression “adjoining owner” means the owner or one of the owners and “adjoining occupier” means the occupier or one of the occupiers of land buildings storeys or rooms adjoining those of the building owner.

Section 87

Metropolitan Building Act 1894

Where lands of different owners adjoin and are unbuilt on at the line of junction and either owner is about to build on any part of the line of junction the following provisions shall have effect:

(1) If the building owner desire to build a party wall on the line of junction he may serve notice thereof on the adjoining owner describing the intended wall.

(2) If the adjoining owner consent to the building of a party wall the wall shall be built half on the land of each of the two owners or in such other position as may be agreed between the two owners.

(3) The expense of the building of the party wall shall be from time to time defrayed by the two owners in due proportion regard being had to the use made and which may be made of the wall by the two owners respectively.

(4) If the adjoining owner do not consent to the building of a party wall the building owner shall not build the wall otherwise than as an external wall placed wholly on his own land.

(5) If the building owner do not desire to build a party wall on the line of junction but desires to build an external wall placed wholly on his own land he may serve notice thereof on the adjoining owner describing the intended wall.

(6) Where in either of the cases aforesaid the building owner proceeds to build an external wall on his own land he shall have a right at his own expense at any time after the expiration of one month from service of the notice to place on the land of the adjoining owner below the level of the lowest floor the projecting footings of the external wall with concrete or other solid substructure thereunder making compensation to the adjoining owner or occupier for any damage occasioned thereby the amount of such compensation if any difference arise to be

determined in the manner in which differences between building owners and adjoining owners are hereinafter directed to be determined.

Where an external wall is built against another external wall or against a party wall it shall be lawful for the district surveyor to allow the footing of the side next such other external or party wall to be omitted.

Section 88
Metropolitan Building Act 1894

The building owner shall have the following rights in relation to party structures (that is to say):

(1) A right to make good underpin or repair any party structure which is defective or out of repair

(2) A right to pull down and rebuild any party structure which is so far defective or out of repair as to make it necessary or desirable to pull it down.

(3) A right to pull down any timber or other partition which divides any buildings and is not conformable with the regulations of this Act and to build instead a party wall conformable thereto.

(4) In the case of buildings having rooms or storeys the property of different owners intermixed a right to pull down such of the said rooms or storeys or any part thereof as are not built in conformity with this Act and to rebuild the same in conformity with this Act.

(5) In the case of buildings connected by arches or communications over public ways or over passages belonging to other persons a right to pull down such of the said buildings arches or communications or such parts thereto as are not built in conformity with this Act.

(6) A right to raise and underpin any party structure permitted by this Act to be raised or underpinned or any external wall built against such party structure upon condition of making good all damage occasioned thereby to the adjoining premises or to the internal finishings and decorations thereof and of carrying up to the requisite height all flues and chimney stacks belonging to the adjoining owner on or against such party structure or external wall.

(7) A right to pull down any party structure which is of insufficient strength for any building intended to be built and to rebuild the same of sufficient strength for the above purpose upon condition of making good all damage occasioned thereby to the adjoining premises or to the internal finishings and decorations thereof.

(8) A right to cut into any party structure upon condition of making good all damage occasioned to the adjoining premises by such operation.

(9) A right to cut away any footing or any chimney breasts jambs or flues projecting or other projections from any party wall or external walls in order to erect an external wall against such party wall or for any other purpose upon condition of making good all damage occasioned to the adjoining premises by such operation.

(10) A right to cut away or take down such parts of any wall or building of an adjoining owner as may be necessary in consequence of such wall or building overhanging the ground of the building owner in order to erect an upright wall against the same on condition of making good any damage sustained by the wall or building by reason of such cutting away or taking down.

(11) A right to perform any other necessary works incident to the connection of a party structure with the premises adjoining thereto but the above rights shall be subject to this qualification that any building which has been erected previously to the date of the commencement of this Act shall be deemed to be conformable with the provisions of this Act if it be conformable with the Acts of Parliament regulating buildings in London before the commencement of this Act.

(12) A right to raise a party fence wall or to pull the same down and rebuild it as a party wall.

Section 89

Metropolitan Building Act 1894

(1) Where a building owner proposes to exercise any of the foregoing rights with respect to party structures the adjoining owner may by notice require the building owner to build on any such party structure such chimney copings jambs or breasts or flues or such piers or recesses or any other like works as may fairly be required for the convenience of such adjoining owner and may be specified in the notice and it shall be the duty of the building owner to comply with such requisition in all cases where the execution of the required works will not be injurious to the building owner or cause to him unnecessary delay in the exercise of his right.

(2) Any difference that arises between a building owner and adjoining owner in respect of the execution of any such works shall be determined in manner in which differences between building owners and adjoining owners are hereinafter to be determined.

Section 90

Metropolitan Building Act 1894

(1) A building owner shall not except with the consent in writing of the adjoining owner and of the adjoining occupiers or in cases where any wall or party structure is dangerous (in which cases the provisions of Part IX of this Act shall apply) exercise any of his rights under this Act in respect of any party fence wall unless at least one month or exercise any of his rights under this Act in relation to any party wall or party structure other than a party fence wall unless at least two months before doing so he has served on the adjoining owner a party wall or party structure notice stating the nature and particulars of the proposed work and the time at which the work is proposed to be commenced.

(2) When a building owner in the exercise of any of his rights under this Part of the Act lays open any part of the adjoining land or buildings he shall at his own expense make and maintain for a proper time a proper hoarding and shoring or temporary construction for protection of the adjoining land or building and the security of the adjoining occupier.

(3) A building owner shall not exercise any right by this Act given to him in such manner or at such time as to cause unnecessary inconvenience to the adjoining owner or to the adjoining occupier.

(4) A party wall or structure notice shall not be available for the exercise of any right unless the work to which the notice relates is begun within six months after the service thereof and is prosecuted with due diligence.

(5) Within one month after receipt of such notice the adjoining owner may serve on the building owner a notice requiring him to build on any such party structure any works to the construction of which he is hereinbefore declared to be entitled.

Section 90(6)
Metropolitan Building Act 1894

(6) The last mentioned notice shall specify the works required by the adjoining owner for his convenience and shall if necessary be accompanied by explanatory plans and drawings.

(7) If either owner do not within fourteen days after the service on him of any notice express his consent thereto he shall be considered as having dissented therefrom and thereupon a difference shall be deemed to have arisen between the building owner and the adjoining owner.

Section 91
Metropolitan Building Act 1894

(1) In all cases (not specifically provided for by this Act) where a difference arises between a building owner and an adjoining owner in respect of any matter arising with reference to any work to which any notice given under this part of this Act relates unless both parties concur in the appointment of one surveyor they shall each appoint a surveyor and the two surveyors so appointed shall select a third surveyor and such one surveyor or three surveyors or any two of them shall settle any matter from time to time during the continuance of any work to which the notice relates in dispute between such building and adjoining owner with power by his or their award to determine the right to do and the time and manner of doing any work and generally any other matter arising out of or incidental to such difference but any time so appointed for doing any work shall not unless otherwise agreed commence until after the expiration of the period by this part of the Act prescribed for the notice in the particular case.

(2) Any award given by such one surveyor or by such three surveyors or by any two of them shall be conclusive and shall not be questioned in any court with this exception that either of the parties to the difference may appeal therefrom to the county court within fourteen days from the date of the delivery of the award and the county court may subject as hereafter in this section mentioned rescind the award or modify it in such manner as it thinks fit.

(3) If either party to the difference make default in appointing a surveyor for ten days after notice has been served on him by the other party to make such appointment the party giving the notice may make the appointment in the place of the party so making default.

(4) The costs incurred in making or obtaining the award shall be paid by such party as the surveyor or surveyors determine.

Section 91(5)
Metropolitan Building Act 1894

(5) If the appellant from any such award, on appearing before the county court declare his unwillingness to have the matter decided by that court and prove to the satisfaction of the judge of that court that in the event of the matter being decided against him he will be liable to pay a sum exclusive of costs exceeding fifty pounds and gives security to be approved by the judge duly to prosecute his appeal and to abide the event thereof all proceedings in the county court shall thereupon be stayed and the appellant may bring an action in the High Court against the other party to the difference.

(6) The plaintiff in such action shall deliver to the defendants an issue whereby the matters in difference between them may be tried and the form of such issue in case of dispute or in the case of non appearance of the defendant shall be settled by the High Court and such action shall be prosecuted and issue tried in the same manner and subject to the same incidents in and subject to which actions are prosecuted and issues tried in other cases within the jurisdiction of the High Court or as near thereto as circumstances admit.

(7) If the parties to any such action agree as to the facts a special case may be stated for the opinion of the High Court and any case so stated may be brought before the Court in like manner and subject to the same incidents in and subject to which other special cases are brought before such Court or as near thereto as circumstances admit and any costs that may have been incurred in the County Court by the parties to such action as is mentioned in this section shall be deemed to be costs incurred in such action, and be payable accordingly.

(8) Where both parties to the difference have concurred in the appointment of one surveyor for the settlement of such difference then if such surveyor refuse or for seven days neglect to act or die or become incapable to act before he has made his award the matters in dispute shall be determined in the same manner as if such single surveyor had not been appointed.

(9) Where each party to the difference has appointed a surveyor for the settlement of the difference and a third surveyor has been selected then if such third surveyor refuse or for seven days neglect to act or before such difference is settled die or become incapable to act the two surveyors shall forthwith select another third surveyor in his place and every third surveyor so selected as last aforesaid shall have the same powers and authorities as were vested in his predecessor.

(10) Where each party to the difference has appointed a surveyor for the settlement of the difference then if the two surveyors so appointed refuse or for seven days after request of either party neglect to select a third surveyor or another third surveyor in the event of the refusal or neglect to act death or incapacity of the third surveyor for the time being a secretary of state may on the application of either party select some fit person to act as third surveyor and every surveyor so selected shall have the same powers and authorities as if he had been selected by the two surveyors appointed by the parties.

(11) Where each party to the difference has appointed a surveyor for the settlement of the difference then if before such difference is settled either surveyor so appointed die or become incapable to act the party by whom such surveyor was appointed may appoint in writing some other surveyor to act in his place and if for the space of seven days after notice served on him by the

other party for that purpose he fail to do so the other surveyor may proceed *ex parte* and the decision of such other surveyor shall be as effectual as if he had been a single surveyor in whose appointment both parties had concurred and every surveyor so to be substituted as aforesaid shall have the same powers and authorities as were vested in the former surveyor at the time of his death or disability as aforesaid.

Section 91(12)
Metropolitan Building Act 1894

(12) Where each party to the difference has appointed a surveyor for the settlement of the difference then if either of the surveyors refuse or for seven days neglect to act the other surveyor may proceed *ex parte* and the decision of such other surveyor shall be as effectual as if he had been a single surveyor in whose appointment both parties had concurred.

Section 92
Metropolitan Building Act 1894

A building owner his servants agents and workmen at all usual times of working may enter and remain on any premises for the purpose of executing and may execute any work which he has become entitled or is required in pursuance of this Act to execute removing any furniture or doing any other thing which may be necessary and if the premises are closed he and they may accompanied by a constable or other officer of the peace break open any fences or doors in order to effect such entry:

Provided that before entering on any premises for the purposes of this section the building owner shall except in the case of emergency give fourteen days' notice of his intention so to do to the owner and occupier and in case of emergency shall give such notice as may be reasonably practicable.

Section 93
Metropolitan Building Act 1894

Where a building owner intends to erect within ten feet of a building belonging to an adjoining owner a building or structure any part of which such ten feet extends to a lower level than the foundations of the building belonging to the adjoining owner he may and if required by the adjoining owner shall (subject as hereinafter provided) underpin or otherwise strengthen the foundations of the said building so far as may be necessary and the following provisions shall have effect:

(1) At least two months' notice in writing shall be given by the building owner to the adjoining owner stating his intention to build and whether he proposes to underpin or otherwise strengthen the foundations of the said building and such notice shall be accompanied by a plan and sections showing the site of the proposed building and the depth to which he proposes to excavate.

(2) If the adjoining owner shall within fourteen days after being served with such notice give a counter notice in writing that he disputes the necessity of or require such underpinning or strengthening a difference shall be deemed to have arisen between the building owner and the adjoining owner.

(3) The building owner shall be liable to compensate the adjoining owner and occupier for any inconvenience loss or damage which may result to them by reason of the exercise of the powers conferred by this section.

(4) Nothing in this section shall relieve the building owner from any liability to which he would otherwise be subject in case of injury caused by his building operations to the adjoining owner.

Section 94
Metropolitan Building Act 1894

An adjoining owner may if he think fit by notice in writing require the building owner (before commencing any work which he may be authorised by this part of this Act to execute) to give such security as may be agreed upon or in case of difference may be settled by the judge of the county court for the payment of all such expenses costs and compensation in respect of the work as may be payable by the building owner.

The building owner may if he thinks fit at any time after service on him of a party wall or party structure requisition by the adjoining owner and before beginning a work to which the requisition relates but not afterwards serve a counter requisition on the adjoining owner requiring him to give such security for payment of the expenses costs and compensation for which he is or will be liable as may be agreed upon or in case of difference may be settled as aforesaid.

If the adjoining owner do not within one month after service of that counter requisition give security accordingly he shall at the end of that month be deemed to have ceased to be entitled to compliance with his party wall or party structure requisition and the building owner may proceed as if no party wall or party structure requisition had been served on him by the adjoining owner.

Section 95

Metropolitan Building Act 1894

(1) As to expenses to be borne jointly by the building owner and adjoining owner:

(a) If any party structure be defective or out of repair the expense of making good underpinning or repairing the same shall be borne by the building owner and adjoining owner in due proportion regard being had to the use that each owner makes or may make of the structure;

(b) If any party structure be pulled down and rebuilt by reason of its being so far defective or out of repair as to make it necessary or desirable to pull it down the expense of such pulling down and rebuilding shall be borne by the building owner and adjoining owner in due proportion regard being had to the use that each owner may make of the structure;

(c) If any timber or other partition dividing a building be pulled down in exercise of the right by this part of this Act vested in a building owner and a party structure be built instead thereof the expense of building such party structure and also of building any additional party structures that may be required by reason of the partition having been pulled down shall be borne by the building owner and adjoining owner in due proportion regard being had to the use that each owner may make of the party structure and to the thickness required for support of the respective buildings parted thereby;

(d) If any rooms or storeys or any parts thereof the property of different owners and intermixed in any building be pulled down in pursuance of the right by this part of this Act vested in a building owner and be rebuilt in conformity with this Act the expense of such pulling down and rebuilding shall be borne by the building owner and adjoining owner in due proportion regard being had to the use that each owner may make of such rooms or storeys;

Section 95(1)(e)
Metropolitan Building Act 1894

(e) If any arches or communications over public ways or over passages belonging to other persons than the owners of the buildings connected by such arches or communications or any parts thereof be pulled down in pursuance of the right by this part of this Act vested in a building owner and be rebuilt in conformity with this Act the expense of such pulling down and rebuilding shall be borne by the building owner and adjoining owner in due proportion regard being had to the use that each owner may make of such arches or communications.

(2) As to expenses to be borne by the building owner:

(a) If any party structure or any external wall built against another external wall be raised or underpinned in pursuance of the power by this part of this Act vested in a building owner the expense of raising or underpinning the same and of making good all damage occasioned thereby and of carrying up to the requisite height all such flues and chimney stacks belonging to the adjoining owner on or against any such party structure or external wall as are by this part of this Act required to be made good and carried up shall be borne by the building owner;

(b) if any party structure which is of proper materials and sound or not so far defective or out of repair as to make it necessary or desirable to pull it down be pulled down and rebuilt by the building owner the expense of pulling down and rebuilding the same and of making good any damage by this part of the Act required to be made good and a fair allowance in respect of the disturbance and inconvenience caused to the adjoining owner shall be borne by the building owner;

(c) If any party structure be cut into by the building owner and the expense of cutting into same and of making good any damage by this part of this Act required to be made good shall be borne by such building owner;

(d) If any footing chimney breast jambs or floor be cut away in pursuance of the powers by this part of this Act vested in a building owner the expense of such cutting away and of making good any damage by this part of this Act required to be made good shall be borne by the building owner;

(e) If any party fence wall be raised for a building the expense of raising such wall shall be borne by the building owner;

(f) If any party fence wall be pulled down and built as a party wall the expense of pulling down such party fence wall and building the same as a party wall shall be borne by the building owner.

If at any time the adjoining owner make use of any party structure or external wall (or any part thereof) raised or underpinned as aforesaid or of any party fence wall pulled down and rebuilt as a party wall (or any part thereof) beyond the use thereof made by him before the alteration there shall be borne by the adjoining owner from time to time a due proportion of the expenses (having regard to the use that the adjoining owner may make thereof):

(i) Of raising or underpinning such party structure or external wall and of making good all such damage occasioned thereby to the adjoining owner and of carrying up to the requisite height all such flues and chimney stacks belonging to the adjoining owner on or against any such party structure or external wall as are by this Part of this Act required to be made good and carried up;

Section 95(2)(f)(ii)
Metropolitan Building Act 1894

(ii) Of pulling down and building such party fence wall as a party wall.

Within one month after the completion of any work which a building owner is by this Part of this Act authorised or required to execute and the expense of which is in whole or in part to be borne by an adjoining owner the building owner shall deliver to the adjoining owner an account in writing of the particulars and expense of the work specifying any deduction to which such adjoining owner or other person may be entitled in respect of old materials or in other respects and every such work shall be estimated and valued at fair average rates and prices according to the nature of the work and the locality and the market price of materials and labour at the time.

Section 97
Metropolitan Building Act 1894

At any time within one month after delivery of the said account the adjoining owner if dissatisfied therewith may declare his dissatisfaction to the building owner by notice in writing served by himself or his agent and specifying his objection thereto and thereupon a difference shall be deemed to have arisen between the parties and shall be determined in manner hereinbefore in this part of this Act provided for the settlement of differences between building and adjoining owners.

Section 98
Metropolitan Building Act 1894

If within the said period of one month the adjoining owner do not declare in the said manner his dissatisfaction with the account he shall be deemed to have accepted the same and shall pay the same on demand to the party delivering the account and if he fail to do so the amount so due may be recovered as a debt.

Section 99

Metropolitan Building Act 1894

Where the adjoining owner is liable to contribute to the expenses of building any party structure then until such contribution is paid the building owner at whose expense the same was built shall stand possessed of the sole property in the structure.

Section 100
Metropolitan Building Act 1894

The adjoining owner shall be liable for all expenses incurred on his requisition by the building owner and in default payment of the same may be recovered from him as a debt.

Section 101

Metropolitan Building Act 1894

Nothing in this Act shall authorise any interference with an easement of light or other easements in or relating to a party wall or take away abridge or prejudicially affect any right of any person to preserve or restore any light or other thing in or connected with a party wall in case of the party wall being pulled down or rebuilt.

Section 3

Metropolitan Building Act 1855

In the Construction of this Act (if not inconsistent with the Context) the following Terms shall have the respective Meanings hereinafter assigned to them; (that is to say,)

"*External Wall*" shall apply to every outer Wall or vertical Enclosure of any Building not being a Party Wall:

"*Party Wall*" shall apply to every Wall used or built in order to be used as a Separation of any Building from any other Building, with a view to the same being occupied by different Persons:

"*Cross Wall*" shall apply to every Wall used or built in order to be used as a Separation of one Part of any Building from another Part of the same Building, such Building being wholly in One Occupation:

"*Party Structure*" shall include Party Walls, and also Partitions, Arches, Floors, and other Structures separating Buildings, Stories or Rooms which belong to different Owners, or which are approached by distinct Staircases or separate Entrances from without:

"*The Base of the Wall*" shall mean the Course immediately above the Footings:

"*Person*" shall include "a Body Corporate".

Section 82

Metropolitan Building Act 1855

In the Construction of the following Provisions relating to Party Structures, such One of the Owners of the Premises separated by or adjoining to any Party Structure as is desirous of executing any Work in respect to such Party Structure shall he called the Building Owner, and the Owner of the other Premises shall be called the Adjoining Owner.

Section 83

Metropolitan Building Act 1855

The Building Owner shall have the following Rights in relation to Party Structures; that is to say,

(1) A Right to make good or repair any Party Structure that is defective or out of repair:

(2) A Right to pull down and rebuild any Party Structure that is so far defective or out of repair as to make it necessary or desirable to pull down the same:

(3) A Right to pull down any Timber or other Partition that divides any Buildings, and is not conformable with the Regulations of this Act, and to build instead a Party Wall conformable thereto:

(4) In the Case of Buildings having Rooms or Stories, the Property of different Owners intermixed, a Right to pull down such of the said Rooms or Stories or any Part thereof as are not built in conformity with this Act, and to rebuild the same in conformity with this Act:

(5) In the Case of Buildings connected by Arches or Communications over public Ways or over Passages belonging to other Persons, a Right to pull down such of the said Buildings, Arches, or Communications, or any Part thereof, as are not built in conformity with this Act, and to rebuild the same in conformity with this Act:

(6) A Right to raise any Party Structure permitted by this Act to be raised, or any External Wall built against such Party Structure, upon Condition of making good all Damage occasioned thereby to the adjoining Premises or to the internal Finishings and Decorations thereof, and of carrying tip to the requisite Height all Flues and Chimney Stacks belonging to the Adjoining Owner on or against such Party Structure or External Wall

Section 83(7)
Metropolitan Building Act 1855

(7) A Right to pull down any Party Structure that is of insufficient Strength for any Building intended to be built, and to rebuild the same of sufficient Strength for the above Purpose, upon Condition of making good all Damage occasioned thereby to the adjoining Premises, or to the internal Finishings and Decorations thereof:

(8) A Right to cut into any Party Structure upon Condition of making good all Damage occasioned to the adjoining Premises by such Operation:

(9) A Right to cut away any Footing or any Chimney Breasts, Jambs, or Flues projecting from any Party Wall, in order to erect an External Wall against such Party Wall, or for any other Purpose, upon Condition of making good all Damage occasioned to the adjoining Premises by such Operation:

(10) A Right to cut away or take down such Parts of any Wall or Building of an Adjoining Owner as may be necessary in consequence of such Wall or Building overhanging the Ground of the Building Owner, in order to erect all upright Wall against the same, on Condition of making good any Damage sustained by the Wall or Building by reason of such cutting away or taking down:

(11) A Right to perform any other necessary Works incident to the Connexion of Party Structure with the Premises adjoining thereto:

But the above Rights shall be subject to this Qualification, that any Building which has been erected previously to the Time of this Act coming into operation shall be deemed to be conformable with the Provisions of this Act, if it is conformable with the Provisions of an Act passed in the Fourteenth Year of

His late Majesty King George the Third, Chapter Seventy-eight, or with the Provisions of the said Act of the Eighth Year of Her present Majesty, Chapter Eighty-four.

Section 84

Metropolitan Building Act 1855

Whenever the Building Owner proposes to exercise any of the foregoing Rights with respect to Party Structures, the Adjoining Owner may require the Building Owner to build on any such Party Structure certain Chimney Jambs, Breasts, or Flues, or certain Piers or Recesses, or any other like Works for the Convenience of such Adjoining Owner-, and it shall be the Duty of the Building Owner to comply with such Requisition in all Cases where the Execution of the required Works will not be injurious to the Building Owner, or cause to him unnecessary inconvenience or unnecessary Delay in the Exercise of his Right; and any Difference that arises between any Building Owner and Adjoining Owner in respect of the Execution of such Works as aforesaid shall be determined in manner in which Differences between Building Owners and Adjoining Owners are hereinafter directed to be determined.

Section 85
Metropolitan Building Act 1855

The following Rules shall be observed with respect to the Exercise by Building Owners and Adjoining Owners of their respective Rights:-

(1) No Building Owner shall, except with the Consent of the Adjoining Owner, or in Cases where any Party Structure is dangerous, in which Cases the Provisions hereby made as to dangerous Structures shall apply, exercise any Right hereby given in respect of any Party Structure, unless he has given at the least Three Months previous Notice to the Adjoining Owner by delivering the same to him personally, or by sending it by Post in a registered Letter addressed to such Owner at his last known Place of Abode:

(2) The Notice so given shall be in Writing or printed, and shall state the Nature of the proposed Work, and the Time at which such Work is proposed to be commenced:

(3) No Building Owner shall exercise any Right hereby given to him in such Manner or at such Time as to cause unnecessary Inconvenience to the Adjoining Owner:

(4) Upon the Receipt of such Notice the Adjoining Owner may require the Building Owner to build, or may himself build on any such Party Structure, any Works to the Construction of which he is hereinbefore mentioned to be entitled:

(5) Any Requisition so made by an Adjoining Owner shall be in Writing or printed, and shall be delivered personally to the Building Owner within One Month after the Date of the Notice being given by him, or be sent by Post in a registered Letter addressed to him at his last known Place of Residence-, It shall specify the Works required by the Adjoining Owner for his Convenience, and shall, if necessary, be accompanied with explanatory Plans and Drawings:

Section 85(6)
Metropolitan Building Act 1855
Continued

(6) If either Owner does not, within Fourteen Days after the Delivery to him of any Notice or Requisition, express his Consent thereto, he shall be considered as having dissented therefrom, and thereupon a Difference shall be deemed to have arisen between the Building Owner and working, the Adjoining Owner:

(7) In all Cases not hereby specially provided for, where a Difference arises between a Building Owner and Adjoining Owner in respect of any Matter arising under this Act, unless both Parties concur in the Appointment of One Surveyor, they shall each appoint a Surveyor, and the Two Surveyors so appointed shall select a Third Surveyor, and such One Surveyor or Three Surveyors, or any Two of them, shall settle any Matter in Dispute between such Building and Adjoining Owner, with Power by his or their Award to determine the Right to do, and the Time and Manner of doing any Work, and generally any other Matter arising out of or incidental to such Difference; but any Time so appointed for doing any Work shall not commence until after the Expiration of such Period of Three Months, as is hereinbefore mentioned:

(8) Any Award given by such One Surveyor, or by such Three Surveyors, or any Two of them, shall be conclusive, and shall not be questioned in any Court, with this Exception, that either of the Parties to the Difference may appeal therefrom to the County Court, within Fourteen Days from the Date of the Delivery of any such Award as aforesaid, and such County Court may, subject as herein-after mentioned, rescind or modify the Award so given in such Manner as it thinks just:

(9) If either Party to the Difference makes default in appointing a Surveyor for Ten Days after Notice has been given to him by the other Party in manner aforesaid to make such Appointment, the Party giving the Notice may make the Appointment in the Place of the Party so making default:

(10) The Costs incurred in obtaining any such Award as aforesaid shall be paid by such Party as such One Surveyor, or Three Surveyors, or any Two of them, may determine:

(11) If the Appellant from any such Award as aforesaid, on appearing before the County Court, declares his Unwillingness to have the Matter decided by such Court, and proves, to the Satisfaction of the Judge of such Court, that, in the event of the Matter being decided against him, he will be liable to pay a Sum, exclusive of Costs, exceeding Fifty Pounds and gives Security, to be approved by such Judge, duly to prosecute his Appeal and to abide the Event aforesaid, or wilfully thereof, all Proceedings in the County Court shall thereupon be stayed; and it shall be lawful for such Appellant to bring an Action in One of Her Majesty's Superior Courts of Law at Westminster against the other Patty to the Difference; and the Plaintiff in such Action shall deliver to the Defendants an Issue or Issues whereby the Matters in difference between them may be tried; and the Form of such Issue or Issues, in case of Dispute, or in case of Nonappearance of the Defendant, shall be settled by the Court in which the Action is brought; and such Action shall be prosecuted and Issue or Issues tried in the same Manner and subject to the same Incidents in and subject to which Actions are prosecuted and Issues tried in other Cases within the Jurisdiction of such Court, or as near thereto as Circumstances admit

Section 85(12)
Metropolitan Building Act 1855

(12) If the Parties to any such Action agree as to the Facts, a special Case may be stated for the Opinion of any such Superior Court as aforesaid, and any Case so stated may be brought before the Court in like Manner and subject to the same Incidents in and subject to which other special Cases are brought before such Court, or as near thereto as Circumstances admit; and any Costs that may have been incurred in the County Court by the Parties to such Action as is mentioned in this Section, shall be deemed to be Costs incurred in such Action, and be payable accordingly.

Section 86
Metropolitan Building Act 1855

Whenever any Building Owner has become entitled, in pursuant of this Act, to execute any Work, it shall be lawful for them, his Servants, Agents, or Workmen, at all usual Times of working, to enter on any Premises for the Purpose of executing and to execute such Work, removing any Furniture, or doing any other Thing that may be necessary, and if such Premises are closed he or they may, accompanied by a Constable or other Officer of the Peace, break open any Doors in order to such Entry, and any Owner or other Person that hinders or obstructs any Workmen employed for any of the Purposes aforesaid, or wilfully damages or inures the said Work, shall incur for each such Offence, a Penalty not exceeding Ten Pounds, to be recovered before a Justice of the Peace.

Section 87
Metropolitan Building Act 1855

Any Adjoining Owner may, if he thinks fit, by Notice in Writing given by himself or his Agent, require the Building Owner before commencing any Work which he may be authorised by this Act to execute, to give such Security as may be agreed upon, or, in case of Difference, may be settled by the Judge of the County Court, for the Payment of all such Costs and Compensation in respect of such Work as may be payable by such Building Owner.

Section 88
Metropolitan Building Act 1855

The following Rules shall be observed as to Expenses in respect of any Party Structure; (that is to say)

As to Expenses to be borne jointly by the Building Owner and Adjoining Owner:

(1) If any Party Structure is defective or out of repair, the Expense of making good or repairing the same shall be borne by the Building Owner and Adjoining Owner in due Proportion, regard being had to the Use that each Owner makes of such Structure:

(2) If any Party Structure is pulled down and rebuilt by reason of its being so far defective or out of repair as to make it necessary or desirable to pull down the same, the Expense of such pulling down and rebuilding shall be borne by the Building Owner and Adjoining Owner in due Proportion, regard being had to the Use that each Owner makes of such Structure:

(3) If any Timber or other Partition dividing any Building is pulled down, in exercise of the Right herein-before vested in a Building Owner, and a Party Structure built instead thereof, the Expense of building such Party Structure, and also of building any additional Party Structures that may be required by reason of such Partition having been pulled down, shall be borne by the Building Owner and Adjoining Owner in due Proportion, regard being had to the Use that each Owner makes of such Party Structure, and to the Thickness required to the respective Buildings parted thereby:

Section 88(4)

Metropolitan Building Act 1855

(4) If any Room or Stories, or any Part of Rooms or Stories, the Property of different Owners, and intermixed in any Building, are pulled down in pursuance of the Right herein-before vested in any Building Owner, and rebuilt it conformity with this Act, the Expense of such pulling down and rebuilding shall be borne by the Building Owner and Adjoining Owner in due Proportion, regard being had to the Use that each Owner makes of such Rooms or Stories:

(5) If any Arches or Communications, ions, or any Parts thereof, are pulled down in pursuance of the Right herein-before vested in any Building Owner, and rebuilt in conformity with this Act, the Expense of such pulling down and rebuilding shall be borne by the Building Owner and Adjoining Owner in due Proportion, regard being had to the Use that each Owner makes of such Arches or Communications:

As to Expenses to be borne by Building Owner:

(6) If any Party Structure or External Wall built against the same is raised in pursuance of the Power herein-before vested in any Building Owner, the Expense of raising the same, and of making good all such Damage, and of carrying up to the requisite Height all such Flues and Chimneys as are hereinbefore required to be made good and carried up, shall be borne by the Building Owner:

(7) If any Patty Structure which is of proper Materials and sound, or not so far defective or out of repair as to make it necessary or desirable to pull down the same, is pulled down and rebuilt by the Building Owner, the Expense of pulling down and rebuilding the same, and of making good all such Damage as is hereinbefore required to be made good, shall be borne by Building Owner is by the Building Owner:

Section 88(8)

Metropolitan Building Act 1855

(8) If any Party Structure is cut into by the Building Owner, the Expense of cutting into the same, and of making good any Damage hereinbefore required to be made good, shall be borne by such Building Owner:

(9) If any Footing, Chimney Breast, Jambs, or Floor is cut away in pursuance of the Powers hereinbefore vested in any Building Owner, the Expense of such cutting away, and of making good any Damage hereinbefore required to be made good, shall be borne by the Building Owner.

Section 89
Metropolitan Building Act 1855

Within One Month after the Completion of any Work which any Building Owner is by this Act authorised or required to execute, and the Expense of which is in whole or in part to be borne by an Adjoining Owner, such Building Owner shall deliver to the Adjoining Owner an Account in Writing of the Expense of the Work, specifying any Deduction to which such Adjoining Owner or other Person may be entitled in respect of old Materials, or in other respects; and every such Work as aforesaid shall be estimated and valued at fair average Rates and Prices, according to the Nature of the Work and the Locality, and the Market Price of Materials and Labour at the Time.

Section 90

Metropolitan Building Act 1855

At any Time within One Month after the Delivery of such Account, the Adjoining Owner, if dissatisfied therewith, may declare his Dissatisfaction to the Party delivering the same, by Notice in Writing given by himself or his Agent, and specifying his Objections thereto; and upon such Notice having been given, a Difference shall be deemed to have arisen between the Parties, and such Difference shall be determined fit manner herein-before provided for the Determination of Differences between Building and Adjoining Owners.

Section 91

Metropolitan Building Act 1855

If within such Period of One Month as aforesaid the Party receiving such Account does not declare in manner aforesaid his Dissatisfaction therewith, he shall be deemed to have accepted the same, and shall pay the same, on Demand, to the Party delivering the Account, and if he fails to do so, the Amount so due may be recovered as a Debt.

Section 92

Metropolitan Building Act 1855

Where the Adjoining Owner is liable to contribute to the Expenses of building any Party Structure, until such Contribution is paid, the Building Owner at whose Expense the same was built shall stand possessed of the sole Property in such Structure.

Section 93
Metropolitan Building Act 1855

Where any Building Owner has incurred any Expenses on the Requisition of an Adjoining Owner, the Adjoining Owner making such Requisition shall be liable for all such Expenses, and in default of Payment, the same may be recovered from him as a Debt.

Section 94

Metropolitan Building Act 1855

Where any Building Owner is, by the Third Part of this Act, liable to make good any Damage he may occasion to the Property of the Adjoining Owner by any Works authorised to be executed by him, or to do any other Thing upon Condition of doing which, his Right to execute such Works is hereby limited to arise, and such Building-Owner fails within a reasonable Time to make good such Damage or to do such Thing, he shall incur a Penalty, to be recovered before a Justice of the Peace, not exceeding Twenty Pounds for each Day during which such Failure continues.

Section 95

Metropolitan Building Act 1855

Where, in pursuance of this Act, any Consent is required to be given, any Notice to be served, or any other Thing to be done by, on, or to any Owner under Disability, such Consent may be given, such Notice may be served, and such Thing may be done by, on, or to the following Persons, on behalf of such Persons under Disability; that is to say,

By, on, or to a Husband, on behalf of his Wife:

By, on, or to a Trustee, on behalf of his Cestuique Trust:

By, on, or to a Guardian or Committee, on behalf of air Infant, Idiot, or Lunatic.

Section 96

Metropolitan Building Act 1855

Where any Consent is required to be given or any other Thing to be done by any Owner in pursuance of this Act, if there is no Owner capable of giving such Consent or of doing such Thing, and no Person empowered by this Act to give such Consent or to do such Thing on behalf of such Owner, or if any Owner so capable, or any Person so empowered, cannot be found, the Judge of the County Court shall have Power to give such Consent, or do or cause to be done such Thing on behalf of such Owner, upon such Terms and subject to such Conditions as he may think fit, having regard alike to the Nature and Purpose of the Subject Matter in respect of which such Consent is to be given, and to the fair Claims of the Parties oil whose Behalf such Consent is to be given; and such Judge shall have Power to dispense with the Service of any Notice which would otherwise be required to be served.

Section 32
London Building Act 1774

Provided nevertheless, That the last-mentioned Clause or Provision relating to Houses and Buildings in Part over public Ways, or having the Rooms or Floors the Property of different Persons, shall not extend to all or any of the Rooms or Chambers in Serjeant's Inn in Chancery Lane, or in any of the four Inns of Court, or to any of the Inns of Chancery, or any other Inns set apart for the Study or Practice of the Law; save and except that the Walls or Divisions between the several Rooms and Chambers in such Inns, belonging to and communicating with each separate and distinct Staircase, shall be deemed and taken to be Party Walls within this Act, and shall be subject to all and every the Regulations and Clauses herein contained relating to other Party Walls within the Limits aforesaid.

Section 33

London Building Act 1774

And whereas it may sometimes happen that no Party Wall or Party Arch can be built upon proper Foundations between such Houses and other Buildings, over public Ways, or having Rooms or Floors the Property of different Persons, lying intermixed, as aforesaid, without pulling down such Houses or Buildings, and laying Parts of each to the others of such Houses or Buildings; and it may happen that the Parties interested therein, or sonic or one of them, will not, or cannot, by reason of some legal Disability, or otherwise, join in building such Party Wall or Party Arches, as aforesaid, or in pulling down such Houses, and laying Parts of each to the other or others of such Houses; in all which Cases, Differences may arise amongst the said several Owners, and the rebuilding the same, and the said Party Walls or Party Arches thereof, may be thereby prevented or delayed, to the great Injury or Inconvenience of such of the Owners as are desirous of rebuilding; For Remedy thereof, and in order to prevent the fatal Effects of Fire, be it enacted by the Authority aforesaid, That, in all and every or any of such Cases, when any Owner or Owners of any such House or other Building within the Limits aforesaid, built over any public Way, or intermixed as aforesaid, shall be desirous of rebuilding such House or other Building, and the Owner or Owners of the adjoining House or Building, or of the other Parts of such intermixed House or Building, shall not be willing, or shall not, by reason of sonic legal Disability, or otherwise, be able to join in such rebuilding, then the Party or Parties, so desirous of rebuilding, shall give Notice, in Writing, to the Owner or Owners of such adjoining House or Houses, or other Buildings, or of the other Parts of such intermixed House or Building, that he, she, or they, so intending to rebuild, will apply to the Court of Mayor and Aldermen of the City of London when such House or other Building, or any Part thereof, is situated within tire said City or tire Liberties thereof, or to the Justices of the Peace for the County of Middlesex, or for the County of Surrey, or for the City and Liberty of Westminster, or for the Liberty of the Tower of London, respectively, within whose Jurisdiction such House or other Building, or any Part thereof, is situated, in their respective General or Quarter Sessions of the Peace, to be next holden, after fourteen Days from the Delivery of such Notice, in order to obtain the Judgment and Determination of the said Court of Mayor and Aldermen, or of the said Court of Sessions (as the Case may be), touching the rebuilding such House or Houses, or other Buildings, or such Party Walls or Party Arches, to be described in such Notice, and for ascertaining the Site of a Party Wall or Party Walls, or the Situation of any Party Arches to be built according to the Directions and Restrictions in this Act contained, by delivering a true Copy of such Notice to the Owner or Owners of such adjoining House or Houses, or other Buildings, or of tire other Parts of such intermixed House or Building; or in case such Owner or Owners shall be Linder the Disability of Coverture, Infancy, Idiocy, or Lunacy, then to the Husband or Husbands of such Owner or Owners under Coverture, or to the Guardians, Trustees, or Committees of such Owners being under the Disability of Infancy, Idiocy, or Lunacy respectively, or by leaving the same at his, her, or their last or usual Place of Abode, or by delivering a tine Copy of such Notice to the Tenant in Possession of such adjoining House or Houses or other Buildings, or of the other Parts of such intermixed House or Building; or in case such House or Building shall be uninhabited, then by fixing such Copy, wrote fair and in a legible Hand, to or upon the Door or some other notorious Part of such adjoining or intermixed House or other Building which shall be uninhabited; and in every such Case, it shall and may be lawful to and for the said Court of Mayor and Aldermen, and to and for the said Court of Sessions respectively (as the Case may be), and they are hereby respectively authorised and required, upon Application to them by the Party or Parties so desirous to rebuild, and upon such Proof of such Notice as they shall deem reasonable, to issue their

Warrant or Warrants, Precept or Precepts, to the Sheriffs of London, or to the Sheriff of the said County of Middlesex, or Sheriff of the said County of Surrey, or Sheriff or Bailiff of the Liberty of his Majesty's Tower of London (as the Case may be), requiring them or him respectively to impanel and return a competent Number of substantial and disinterested Persons, qualified to serve on Juries, within the respective Distances to which they are summoned, not less than twenty-four, nor more than thirty-six; and out of such Persons so to be impanelled, summoned, and returned, a Jury of twelve Persons shall be drawn by some Person, by the said Court of Mayor and Aldermen, or Court of Sessions respectively appointed, in such Manner as Juries are directed to be drawn for the Trial of Issues joined in his Majesty's Courts of Record at Westminster, by an Act, made in the third Year of the Reign of his late Majesty King George the Second (entitled, An Act for the better Regulation of Juries); which Persons so to be impanelled, summoned, and returned, are hereby required to come and appear before the said Court of Mayor and Aldermen, or before the said Court of Sessions for the said County of Middlesex, or County of Surly or City and Liberty of Westminster, or the Liberty of his Majesty's Tower of London (as the Case may be), at such Time and Place as in such Warrant or Warrants, Precept or Precepts, shall be appointed, and there to attend from Day to Day, until discharged by the Court; and all Parties concerned shall and may have their lawful Challenges against any of the said Jury, but shall not be at Liberty to challenge the Array; and the said Court of Mayor and Aldermen, and any of the said Courts of Sessions, for the said County of Middlesex, or Surrey, or City and Liberty of Westminster, or Liberty of the Tower of London, is and are hereby authorised and impowered, by Preceptor Precepts, from Time to Time, as Occasion may require, to call before them respectively all and every Person and Persons who shall be thought proper or necessary to be examined as a Witness or

Witness before them, on Oath, concerning the Premises; and either of the said Courts, if they think fit, shall and may likewise authorise the said Jury to view the Place or Places in question, in such Manner as they shall direct, and shall have Power to command such Jury, and all such Witnesses and Parties as shall be necessary or proper to attend, until all such Affairs for which they are summoned shall be concluded; and the said Jury, upon their Oaths (which Oaths, as also the Oaths to Persons called upon to give Evidence, the said Courts are hereby respectively impowered and required to administer), shall inquire and try, and determine by their Verdict, whether the Premises, in any of the Cases aforesaid, ought to be rebuilt or not; and if the same ought to be rebuilt, shall award and determine the Site of a Party Wall or Party Walls, and also what Party Arches may be necessary over or under any Rooms of such House or Houses, or other Buildings, so intended to be rebuilt, or shall ascertain the Quantity of the Soil or Ground or other Parts of the Premises (if any) necessary to be laid to or taken from the House of the Person or Persons desirous to rebuild, permitting such Person or Persons to erect a Party Wall or Party Walls, Party Arch or Party Arches; and shall ascertain and award what (if any) Compensation should be made, and paid, by either or any of the said Parties in Difference to the other or others of them, in lieu of the lessening either of the said Houses or other Buildings by such Party Wall or Party Walls, Party Arch or Party Arches, or as a Satisfaction for such other Injury (if any) as shall be done, or occasioned thereby to any or either of the said Parties; and shall also ascertain and award what Proportion of the Expellee of Building such Party Wall or Party Walls, Party Arch or Party Arches, shall, when the same are so built, be repaid by either or any of the Parties in Difference to the Person or Persons so rebuilding as aforesaid: And the said Court of Mayor and Aldermen, and the said Court of Sessions respectively, shall give Judgment according to such Verdict, as well for determining the Site of such intended Party Wall or Party Walls, Party Arch or Party Arches, as also for such Sum or Sums of Money (if any) so assessed by the said Jury, and likewise for such Proportion of the Expense of building such Party Wall or Party Walls, Party Arch or Party Arches, so sound or awarded by the said Jury, to be repaid to the Person or Persons who shall rebuild or shall have rebuilt the same; and shall and may (if they see fit) award to either of the Parties such Costs as they shall deem reasonable; which Verdict or Verdicts, and the Judgment, Order, or Determination thereupon, shall be binding and conclusive against all and every Person and Persons, Bodies Politic and Corporate, claiming any Estate, Right, Title, Trust, Use, or Interest in, to, or out of the said Premises, or any Part thereof, either in Possession, Reversion, Remainder, or Expectancy, as also against (the King's most Excellent Majesty, his Heirs and Successors, and against Infants and Issue unborn, Persons in Reversion or Remainder, Lunatics, Idiots, and Femes-covert, and Persons under any other legal Incapacity or Disability, and against all Trustees and Cestuique Trusts, his, her, and their Successors, Heirs, Executors, and Administrators, and against all other Persons whomsoever: And all and every the said Verdicts, Judgments, Orders, and Determinations, and all other Proceedings of the said Court of Mayor and Aldermen, and Court of Sessions, so to be made, given, and pronounced, as aforesaid, shall be, by the Town Clerk of the City of London, or by the Clerk of the Peace for the said County of Middlesex or Surrey, or the City and Liberty of Westminster, or the proper Officer of the Liberty of the said Tower of London (as the Case may be), entered and filed as of Record of the said Court where such Proceedings shall have been had (for the Entry and Filing whereof, and for every order of Court, and Copy thereof, the said Town Clerk, or Clerk of the Peace, or other proper Officer, shall be paid after the Rate of Twelve-pence for every one hundred Words, and no more); and each of them, the said Town Clerk, and

Clerk of the Peace, or other proper Officer respectively, is hereby empowered and required to make and deliver to any Person requiring the same, an Exemplification, under his Hand and Seal, of any such Verdict, Judgment, Order, and Determination, being paid for the same after the Rate of Twelve-pence for every one hundred Words; and every such Exemplification shall and may be taken and read as Evidence in all Courts of Law and Equity whatever: And after the Expiration of fourteen Days from and after the obtaining such Judgment, and Payment, or Tender, in Manner hereinafter directed, of the Sum or Sums of Money (if any) thereby assessed or awarded, or, where no Sum of Money shall be so assessed or awarded, after the Expiration of fourteen Days from and after the obtaining such Judgment, the Person or Persons who shall have applied for, and obtained such Judgment, his, her, or their Heirs, Executors, or Administrators, Servants, or Workmen, shall and may pull down his, her, or their own House or other Building, and rebuild the same, in the Manner so ascertained by such Judgment; and to that End shall and may, in the Presence of a Constable or Headborough, or other Officer of the Peace, after the End of fourteen Days after such Judgment, Order, and Determination, shall have been obtained, enter upon the Site of the Ground so ascertained for a Party Wall or Party Walls, Party Arch or Party Arches, and into the House or other Building (if any be) adjoining to the House or Party Wall or Party Walls, Party Arch. or Party Arches, intended to be rebuilt, at any 'lime between the Hours of Six in the Morning and Seven in the Afternoon (Sundays excepted); and if the outer Door of such House or other Building be shut, and the Occupier, or any other Person therein, refuse to open the same, being thereunto required, or if such House or other Building be empty and unoccupied, shall and may break open such outer Door, and remove to some other Part of the same Premises, or in case there be no Room on the Premises sufficient for that Purpose, to remove to any other Place, any Goods, Furniture,

Section 33
London Building Act 1774
Continued

Shelves, or other Thing obstructing the building of such intended Party Wall or Party Walls, Party Arch or Party Arches, or the pulling down any Wall, Partition, or other Thing necessary to be pulled down and removed, in order to the building such intended Party Wall or Party Walls, Party Arch or Party Arches; and from and after such Entry as aforesaid, and at all usual Times of working, it shall be lawful for the Builder or Builders employed to erect such intended Party Wall or Party Walls, Party Arch or Party Arches, and his and their Servants, and all others employed by him or them, to enter into and upon the Premises, and abide therein the usual Times of working, for the shoring up the said House or other Building so broke into or entered upon, and for taking down and removing any Party Wall or Party Walls, Partition, Wainscot, or other Thing necessary to be taken down and removed for the Purpose aforesaid, and to build such intended Party Wall or Party Walls, Party Arch or Party Arches: And if any such Owner or Occupier, or other Person or Persons, shall in any Manner hinder or obstruct any Workman or Workmen employed for any of the Purposes aforesaid, or wilfully damage or injure the said Works, every such Owner or Occupier, or other Person so offending, shall, for every such Offence, forfeit and pay the Sum of ten Pounds; to be levied, recovered, and applied, as the several Penalties of ten Pounds hereinafter mentioned are directed to be levied, recovered, and applied.

Section 34
London Building Act 1774

Provided also, and it is hereby further enacted, That within ten Days after such Party Wall or Party Walls, Party Arch or Party Arches, shall be so built, the Person or Persons who shall have rebuilt the same, his, her, or their Executors, Administrators, or Assigns, shall leave a true Account hi Writing of the Expense of building the same with the Party or Parties so awarded by the Jury as aforesaid to contribute to the Expense thereof, or at his, her, or their last or usual Place of Abode; or, in case such Party or Parties be under Coverture, to her or their respective Husbands; or if Infants, Idiots, or Lunatics, then to their respective Guardians, Trustees, or Committees; or in the Case of any Body Corporate being so awarded to contribute as aforesaid, then to the Mayor or other Officer of such Corporation; who shall pay to the Person or Persons who shall have rebuilt such Party Wall or Party Walls, Party Arch or Party Arches as aforesaid, his, her, or their Executors, Administrators, or Assigns, the Proportion of the Expense of building the same so awarded by the said Jury as aforesaid, within twenty-one Days after Demand thereof; or, in case the same be not so paid, it shall be lawful for the Tenant or Occupier of the House or Building so chargeable therewith to pay the same, and to deduct the Money so paid out of the next Rent which shall become due to the Owner or Owners of such House or Building; or the same may be recovered from the Party or Parties so awarded to pay the same by Action of Debt, Bill, Plaint, or Information, in any of his Majesty's Courts of Record at Westminster, with double Costs of Suit.

Section 35

London Building Act 1774

Provided always, and it is hereby further enacted, That all the Powers and Authorities by this Act vested in the Court of Mayor and Aldermen of the City of London, may be lawfully exercised by the Court of Mayor and Aldermen of the said City, to be holden in the Outer Chamber of the Guildhall of the said City, according to the Custom of the said City.

Section 36
London Building Act 1774

Provided always, and be it further enacted by the Authority aforesaid, That upon every Application to the General Quarter Sessions of the Peace for the said County of Surrey, for or concerning any Matter to be by such Quarter Sessions ordered, directed, or done, in pursuance of this Act, the Jury (if any) to be impanelled, and all Parties required to attend the Quarter Sessions for the said County, pursuant to such Application, shall be impanelled and required to attend at some General or Special Adjournment of the said Quarter Sessions, within six Weeks next after such Application; which said Adjournment shall be to some convenient Place in the Borough of Southwark, in the said County, to be appointed by the Justices in the said Session; and that, from Time to Time, every further Meeting of the said Sessions, for any Thing to be done upon such Application, shall be appointed at, or within the Space of three Weeks from the last Meeting; which Adjournment and Adjournments the Justices of the Peace for the said County of Surrey, and every of them, are hereby empowered and required to make and hold, from Time to Time, as there shall be Occasion.

Section 37

London Building Act 1774

And be it further enacted by the Authority aforesaid, That it shall and may be lawful to and for the said Court of Mayor and Aldermen, and to and for any or either of the aforesaid Courts of Sessions (as the Case may be), and they are hereby empowered and required, from Time to Time, to impose any reasonable Fine or Fines on any of the said Sheriffs or Sheriff, or their or his Deputy or Deputies, making, Default in the Premises, and on any of the Persons who shall be summoned and returned on such Jury, and shall not appear at the Time and Place in such Summons specified, or, appearing, shall refuse to be sworn on Such Jury, or to give his or their Verdict, or in any Manner wilfully neglecting his or their Duty therein, contrary to the true Intent and Meaning of this Act; and on any of the Persons having Notice to attend to give Evidence touching the Premises, who shall not attend, or attending shall refuse to be sworn, examined, and give Evidence; and from Time to Time, in Default of Payment thereof on Demand, to levy such Fine or Fines in such Manner as other Fines set by the said Courts respectively have been usually levied; so that no Fine shall exceed the Sum of ten Pounds upon any one Person for any one Offence; and such Fine or Fines, when so received, or levied and recovered, shall be applied to and for the Use of the Person or Persons so applying to the said Court of Mayor and Aldermen, or to the said Courts of Sessions (as the Case may be), and to and for no other Use or Purpose whatsoever; and if such Person or Persons, having Notice to attend and give Evidence as aforesaid, shall not attend and give Evidence accordingly, having had ten Days previous Notice in Writing thereof, under the Hands of the Party on whose Behalf such Evidence shall be wanted, his Guardian, Trustee, Committee, Attorney, or Agent, and having been tendered his reasonable Charges and Expenses for such Attendance, he, she, or they, so neglecting or refusing to give Evidence, shall be liable to an Action on the Case, to be brought against him, her, or them respectively by the Party or Parties on whose Behalf any such Notice to attend as aforesaid shall have been given; in which the Plaintiff or Plaintiffs shall recover their Damages occasioned by such Non-attendance, with full Costs of Suit; and such and no other Justification or Excuse shall be allowed for Non-attendance, as is by Law allowable for the Non-attendance of Witnesses legally summoned to appear and give Evidence on Trials of Issues joined in any of his Majesty's Courts of Record at Westminster: Provided, the Court where such Witness or Witnesses shall appear may (if they shall think fit) order such further Sum to be paid to such Witness or Witnesses respectively for their Attendance on such Courts respectively, as to them shall seem reasonable, in proportion to the Time such Witness or Witnesses shall attend; and such Witness or Witnesses shall not be compelled to give Evidence before such further Sum or Sums (if any), as shall be so ordered, shall be paid to them respectively.

Section 38
London Building Act 1774
Continued

And whereas it may happen that Party Walls or Party Arches, or Party Fence-walls, built or to be built within the Limits aforesaid, may be defective, or so far out of Repair as to render it necessary to pull down and rebuild the same, or some Part or Parts thereof, as well when both or either of the adjoining Houses or other Buildings may not require to be rebuilt, as when the said Houses or Buildings, or one of them, may require to be rebuilt;' be it enacted by the Authority aforesaid, That from and after the said twenty-fourth Day of June, every owner of any House or Building within Limits aforesaid, who shall think it necessary to repair, pull down, or rebuild any Party Wall or Party Fence-wall, or any Part or Parts thereof, between any such House or Building, or the Ground thereto adjoining, and the next adjoining House or Building, or the Ground thereto adjoining, shall (in case the Owner or Owners of such adjoining House, Building, or Ground, will not, or by reason of any legal Disability, or otherwise, cannot agree, touching the repairing, or pulling down or rebuilding, the same) give three Months Notice in Writing to the Owner, if he is known, and can be met with, or if such Owner or Owners be under Coverture, to her or their Husbands respectively, or if under the Disability of Infancy, Idiocy, or Lunacy, to the Guardian or Guardians, Trustee or Trustees, Committee or Committees, of such Infant, Idiot, or Lunatic respectively, or otherwise to the Occupier of such adjoining House, Building, or Ground, of such his or her Intention to repair, or pull down, such Party Wall, Party Arch, or Party Fence-wall, or any Part thereof, by delivering a Copy of such Notice to such Owner or Occupier, or other Person or Persons as aforesaid, or by leaving the same at his, her, or their last or usual Place of Abode, or, if such adjoining House or Building be unoccupied, by fixing a Copy of such Notice on the Door of such last-mentioned House or Building; which Notice shall be in the Form or to the Effect following:

'APPREHENDING the Party Wall, Party Arch, or Party Fence-wall, or some Part thereof (as the Case shall be), between the House or Building, or Ground (as the Case shall be) thereto adjoining, situate inhabited or occupied by and my House or Building, or Ground (as the Case shall be) adjoining thereto, to be so far out of Repair as to render it necessary to repair or pull down and rebuild the same, or some Part thereof: Take Notice, that I intend to have the said Party Wall, Party Arch, or Party Fence- wall (as the Case shall be), surveyed, pursuant to an Act of Parliament made in the fourteenth Year of the Reign of King George the Third; and that I have appointed of and of my Surveyors, to meet at in (being at some Place within the Limits aforesaid), on my Behalf, on the Day of next, at of the Clock in the of the same Day (being between the Hours of Six in the Morning and Six in the Afternoon): And I do hereby require and call upon you to appoint two other Surveyors or able Workmen on your Part, to meet them at the Time and Place aforesaid, to view the said Party Wall, Party Arch, or Party Fence-wall (as the Case shall be), and to certify the State and Condition thereof, and whether the same, or any Part thereof, ought to be repaired or pulled down and rebuilt. Dated this Day of '

And every such Owner, if he is known, and can be met with, or, in case such Owner be under any Disability, as aforesaid; then such Person or Persons, as aforesaid, to whom such Notice shall be so given, or otherwise the Occupier to whom such Notice shall be so given, shall appoint two Surveyors or able Workmen to meet at the Time and Place in such Notice mentioned; and they, together with the, two Surveyors or Workmen named by the Party giving such Notice, and whose Names shall be expressed in such Notice, may view such Party Wall, Party Arch, or Party Fence-wall, and certify the

Section 38
London Building Act 1774
Continued

State and Condition thereof, and whether the same, or any Part thereof, ought to be repaired, or pulled down and rebuilt; and such Surveyors, so respectively named, as aforesaid, or, in case the Owner or Occupier of such adjoining House or Building, or such other Persons, as aforesaid, having Notice, as aforesaid, shall refuse or neglect to name such two Surveyors or able Workmen, according to such Notice, then the two Surveyors or Workmen named in such Notice together with two other Surveyors or able Workmen, also to be named by the Party giving such Notice, as aforesaid, shall and may, within six Days after the Time appointed in such Notice, view the Party Wall, Party Arch, or Party Fence-wall, intended to be repaired or pulled down; and shall certify, in Writing, under their Hands, to the said Court of Mayor and Aldermen, or to the said Justices of the Peace in their next General or Quarter Sessions of the Peace respectively (as the Case may be), the State and Condition of such Party Wall, Party Arch, or Party Fence-wall, and whether the same, or any Part thereof, ought to be repaired, or pulled down and rebuilt: And in case the major Part of the Surveyors or Workmen, appointed in Manner aforesaid to view such Party Wall, Party Arch, or Party Fence-wall, so intended to be repaired, or pulled down, shall not, within the Space of one Month next after such Appointment, sign such Certificate in Writing; then, and in every such Case, it shall and may be lawful to and for any one or more of his Majesty's Justices of the Peace for the said City of London or County of Middlesex or Surrey, or City and Liberty of Westminster, or Liberty of his Majesty's Tower of London (as the Case shall be), and such one or more Justice or Justices is and are hereby authorised and required, upon Application to him or them for that Purpose by the Party giving such Notice, as aforesaid, to name and appoint one other able Surveyor or Workman to be added to the Surveyors or Workmen, appointed as aforesaid; and all the said Surveyors or Workmen so appointed, or the major Part of them, shall meet for that

Purpose (six Days Notice having been given to or left at the Dwellinghouse of each and every of them of such intended Meeting), and shall view the Party Wall, Party Arch, or Party Fence-wall, so proposed to be repaired or pulled down: And, in case the. major Part of such Surveyors or Workmen, appointed in Manner aforesaid, shall certify, in Writing under their Hands, that the Party Wall, Party Arch, or Party Fence-wall, described in such Notice, or any Part thereof, is decayed and ruinous, or is not sufficiently secure against Fire, if any should happen, and that the same ought to be repaired or pulled down; then, within three Days next after such Certificate made by such major Part of the said Surveyors or Workmen, as aforesaid, a Copy thereof shall be delivered to the Owner or Occupier, Owners or Occupiers of, or lost at such adjoining House or Building, or fixed on the Door thereof, in case the same be unoccupied; and such Certificate shall be immediately filed with the Clerk of the Peace in the City, County, or Liberty where such Wall or Arch is situate, paying such Clerk one Shilling for filing thereof, and no more: And such last-mentioned Owner or Occupier, Owners or Occupiers, shall and may (if he, she, or they, think fit) appeal from or against such Certificate to the next General or Quarter Sessions to be holden for the City, County, or Place (as the Case may be); and the Justices, at the said General or Quarter Sessions, to which such Appeals shall be made, shall summon before them one or more of such Surveyors or Workmen, and such other Person or Persons as they think tit, and shall examine the Matter upon Oath, which Oath or Oaths they are hereby empowered to administer; and upon such Examination or Examinations, the said Justices are hereby authorised and required to make such Order or Orders in the Premises as they in their Discretions shall think to be just and reasonable; which Order or Orders shall be entered and filed of Record by the Clerk of the Peace for the City, County, or Place (as the Case may be), in like Manner as the Judgments of any Court of Sessions concerning intermixed Property are hereinbefore directed to be entered and filed of Record; and the Determination of the said Justices shall be final and conclusive to all Parties, without any Appeal from the same: And, on Default of appealing to such next General or Quarter Sessions, as aforesaid; or if, upon any Appeal, there be no Order made to the contrary; then, and in every such Case, and not otherwise, it shall be lawful for the Party intending to repair, or pull down and rebuild, such Party Wall, Party Arch, or Party Fence-wall, as aforesaid, after the Expiration of fourteen Days after delivering or leaving the Copy of such Certificate, as aforesaid; or after the, Determination of such Appeal, as aforesaid, to cause such Party Wall, Party Arch, or Party Fence-wall, or any Parts thereof, to be repaired or pulled down, and to have and exercise the like Power of Entry into or upon the adjoining House or Houses, Building or Buildings, or of breaking open the same, in the Presence of a Peace Officer, in case the same be unoccupied, or be refused to be opened, and of removing Wainscot, Shelves, Furniture, and other Things, and of shoring up the said adjoining House or Houses, Building or Buildings, as is given or allowed to the Owners of intermixed Houses or Buildings in and by this Act; and shall and may erect and build a new Party Wall or Party Walls, Party Arch or Party Arches, or any Part or Parts thereof, of such Materials, and of such Thickness and Height, and in such Manner, and subject to such Restrictions and Directions, as are in and by this Act prescribed.

Section 39
London Building Act 1774

And whereas several old Houses and other Buildings of the First, Second, and Third Rate or Class of Building within the Limits aforesaid, have, instead of Party Walls of the respective Thicknesses hereinbefore directed for the same, between such Houses or other Buildings and the adjoining Houses or Buildings, Party Walls, not being of greater Thickness than one Brick and an Half in Length, or thirteen Inches, from the Foundation to the Ground Floor thereof, or than one Brick in Length, or eight Inches and an Half, from thence to the Coping thereof: And whereas Disputes may arise concerning the pulling down such old Party Walls, and concerning the building Party Walls agreeable to the Rules and Directions herein contained, in the Place and Stead of such old Party Walls, whenever the Owner or Owners of any or either of the Houses or Buildings adjoining to any such Party Walls may be desirous to rebuild any such House, or rebuild any such House or Building of the First, Second, or Third Rate or Class of Building, or so much thereof as may subject the same, or the Party Walls thereto, to the Rules and Regulations contained in this Act; be it enacted by the Authority aforesaid, That if the Owner or Owners of any House or Building of the First, Second, or Third Rate or Class of Building, to which any such old Party Wall belongs, shall be desirous of pulling down and rebuilding such House or Building, or so much thereof, as aforesaid, and of such his, her, or their Desire shall give three Months Notice, in Writing, to the Owner or Owners, Occupier or Occupiers, of the next adjoining House or Building of his, her, or their intention, in three Months from the Date thereof, to pull down such Party Wall, and in Stead thereof, to build a Party Wall agreeable to this Act of Parliament; then, and in that Case, from and after the Expiration of the three Months expressed in such Notice, it shall be lawful for the Owner of such House and Building, so intended to be rebuilt, to pull down the said Party Wall, and to have and exercise the like Power of entering into and upon the said adjoining House or Building, or of breaking open

Section 39
London Building Act 1774
Continued

the same, in the Presence of a Peace Officer, in case the same be unoccupied, or be refused to be opened, and of removing any Wainscot, Shelves, Furniture, or other Things, and of shoring, up the said adjoining House or Building, as by this Act is given and allowed to the Owners of intermixed Houses or Buildings; and shall and may, in the Place and Stead of every such old Party Wall, build a new Party Wall, of such Materials, Thickness, and Height, and in such Manner, and subject to such Restrictions and Directions, as are in and by this Act prescribed.

Section 40
London Building Act 1774

And whereas several old Houses, or other Buildings, within the Limits aforesaid, have, instead of a Party Wall between such House or other Building, or between such Houses or other Buildings and the Houses or other Buildings and Ground adjoining thereto, one Timber or Wood Partition, or two old Timber or Wood Partitions, with or without Brick Noggin, in one or more of the Stories thereof, one belonging to each House or other Building: And whereas Disputes may arise concerning the pulling down such Partitions, and the Wall or Walls under or over the same, if any such there be, and concerning the building Party Walls, agreeable to the Rules and Directions herein contained, in the Place and Stead of such Partition or Fence, whenever it may be expedient to rebuild any such House or Building, or so much thereof as may subject the same, and the Partitions abutting on file same, to the Rules and Regulations contained in this Act;' be it enacted by the Authority aforesaid, That if the Owner or Owners of any House or Building to which any such Timber or Wood Partition or Partitions, or Wooden Fence belongs, shall be desirous of pulling down and rebuilding such House or Building, or so much thereof as aforesaid, and of such his, her, or their Desire, shall give three Months Notice to the Owner or Owners, Occupier or Occupiers, of the next adjoining House or Building of his, her, or their Intention to pull down such Timber or Wood Partition or Partitions after the End of three Months after the Date of such Notice, and instead thereof to build a Party Wall. or Party Walls, agreeable to this Act of Parliament; then, and in that Case, from and after the Expiration of the three Months expressed in such Notice, it shall be lawful for the Owner of such House or Building so to be rebuilt, to pull down the said Partition or Partitions, and the Wall or Walls under or over the same, if any such there be, and the said Wooden Fence or Fences, and to have and exercise the like Power of Entry into and upon the said adjoining House or Building and Ground, or of breaking open the same in the Presence of a Peace

Section 40
London Building Act 1774
Continued

Officer, in case the same be unoccupied, or be refused to be opened, and of removing, any Wainscot, Shelves, Furniture, or other Things, and of shoring up the said adjoining House or Building, as by this Act is given and allowed to the Owners of intermixed Houses or Buildings; and shall and may, in the Place and Stead of such Partition or Partitions, and of the Wall or Walls under or over the same, if any such there be, or of such Wooden Fence or Fences, build a new Party Wall or Party Walls, of such Materials, Thickness, and Height, and in such Manner, and subject to such Restrictions and Directions, as are in and by this Act prescribed.

Section 41
London Building Act 1774

And be it further enacted by the Authority aforesaid, That the Person or Persons, at whose Expense any Party Wall or Party Arch shall be built agreeably to the Directions of this Act, shall be reimbursed by the Owner or Owners who shall be entitled to the improved Rent of the adjoining Building or Ground, and who shall, at any Time, make use of such Party Wall or Party Arch, a Part of the Expense of building the same, in the Proportion after mentioned; that is to say, If the adjoining Building then erected, or afterwards to be erected, be of the same Rate or Class of Building as, or superior to, the Building belonging to the Person or Persons at whose Expense the said Party Wall was built, then the Owner or Occupier of such adjoining Building or Ground shall pay one Moiety of the Expense of building so much of the said Party Wall or Party Arch as such Owner or Occupier shall make use of; and if the adjoining Building then erected, or afterwards to be erected, be of an inferior Rate or Class of Building, then the Owner or Occupier of such adjoining Building or Ground shall pay a Sum of Money equal one Moiety of the Expense of building a Party Wall or Party Arch of the Thickness by this Act required for the Rate or Class of Building whereof such adjoining Building shall be, and of the Height and Breadth of so much of the said Party Wall or Party Arch as such Owner or Occupier shall make use of: And, in the mean time, and until such Moiety or other proportional Part of the Expense of building such Party Wall or Party Arch be so paid, the sole Property of such whole Party Wall or Party Arch, and of the whole Ground whereon the said Party Wall shall stand, shall be vested entirely in the Person or Persons at whose Expense the same shall be built: And such Moiety, or other proportional Part of the Expense of building such Party Wall or Party Arch shall be so paid to the Person or Persons at whose Expense the same shall be built, or in whom the Property thereof shall be vested at the Times hereinafter mentioned; that is to say, in respect of every such Party Wall to any House or Building whereunto, at the Time of building the

Section 41
London Building Act 1774
Continued

same, no other House or Building was adjoining, so soon as such Party Wall shall be first cut into or made use of; and in respect of every such Party Wall or Party Arch as shall be built against, or adjoining to, any other House or Building, so soon as such Party Wall or Party Arch shall be completely built and finished: And in respect of such last-mentioned Party Wall or Party Arch, the Owner or Occupier of such adjoining House or Building shall, together with such proportional Part of the Expense of building such Party Wall or Party Arch, also pay a like proportional Part of all other Expenses which shall be necessary to the pulling down the old Party Wall, or Timber or Wood Partition, and the Whole of all the reasonable Expenses of shoring up such adjoining House or Building, and of removing any Goods, Furniture, or other Things, and of pulling down any Wainscot or Partition, and also all such Costs, if any, as may have been awarded by the said Court of Mayor and Aldermen, or Court of Sessions, as aforesaid; but not any Part of the Expense of pulling down and clearing away any such old Party Wall or Party Arch, or old Partition, if any such there was: And it is hereby directed, that the Expense of building such Party Wall or Party Arch shall be estimated after the Rate of seven Pounds fifteen Shillings by the Rod, for the new Brickwork, deducting thereout after the Rate of twenty-eight Shillings by the Rod for the Materials (if any) of so much of the old Wall or Arch as did belong to such adjoining Building or Ground, and also after the Rate of Two-pence by the Cubical Foot for the Materials (if any) of so much of the old Timber Partition as did belong to such adjoining Building or Ground: And that within ten Days after such Party Wall or Party Arch shall be so built, or so soon after as conveniently may be, such First Builder or Builders shall leave, at such adjoining House or Building, a true Account, in Writing, of the Number of Rods in such Party Wall or Party Arch for which the Owner or Owners of such adjoining Building or Ground shall be liable to pay, and of the Deduction which such Owner or

Owners shall be entitled to make thereout, on account of such Materials, and also an Account of such other Expenses and Costs as aforesaid; whereupon it shall be lawful for the Tenant or Occupier of such adjoining Building or Ground to pay one Moiety, or such proportional Part, as aforesaid, to such First Builder or Builders for (the same, and also for shoring and supporting such adjoining Building as aforesaid, and for all such other Expenses as are hereinbefore directed to be paid by the Owner or Owners of such adjoining Building or Ground, and to deduct the same out of the Rent which shall become due from him or her to such Owner or Owners, under whom he or she holds the same respectively, until he or she shall be reimbursed the same: And in case the same be not paid within twenty-one Days next after Demand thereof, then the same shall and may be recovered, together with full Costs of Suit, of and from such Owner or Owens, by Action of Debt, or on the Case, in any of his Majesty's Courts of Record at Westminster; wherein no Essoin, Protection, or Wager of Law, or more than one Importance, shall be allowed: And if the Plaintiff or Plaintiffs, in any such Action, shall, three Calendar Months at the least before the Commencement thereof, give Notice in Writing to the Person or Persons against whom such Action is intended to be brought, of his, her, or their Intention to bring the same, or leave the same at his, her, or their last or usual Place of Abode, and shall in such Notice specify the Sum for which it is to be brought, and also annex to such Notice a Bill of the just and true Particulars of the Expenses and Charges with which the intended Defendant or Defendants is or are to be charged; then such Plaintiff or Plaintiffs, if he, she, or they, recover the full Sum specified in such Notice, shall also recover and be entitled to Double Costs of Suit, and shall have and be entitled to the like Remedies for Recovery thereof, as are usually given for Costs in other Cases of Costs at Law.

Section 42
London Building Act 1774

And be it further enacted by the Authority aforesaid, That every Party Wall hereafter to be built, and every Addition which shall be made thereto, or to any Party Wall which is already built or begun, shall be built agreeable to the Directions herein contained concerning the Party Wall of the highest Rate or Class of Building to which such Party Wall shall adjoin, when such Additions are completed; and that no Party Wall now built, or hereafter to be built, shall, after the same and the Buildings adjoining thereto is and are completed, be raised, unless the same when raised be of the full Thickness such Party Wall is of in the Storey next under the Roof of the highest adjoining Building; nor shall any Party Wall hereafter be raised, unless the same can be done with Safety to such Wall, and the several Buildings adjoining thereto; but all such Party Walls as will, when raised, be of the Materials, Heights, and Thicknesses hereinbefore required, or as can be safely raised, may, together with the Shaft or Shafts of the Chimneys belonging thereto, be raised by and at the Expense of the Proprietor or Occupier of any Building, to which the same belong, to any Height he, she, or they, shall think proper; but if the Proprietor or Occupier of any Building adjoining to the said Party Wall and Chimney Shafts, shall make use of any Part of such Party Wall and Chimney Shaft, other than the Use the makes of the Chimney Flues therein, which shall be so raised, then such Person so making use thereof, for the Part so used, shall be chargeable with a proportionable Share of the Expense of raising such Party Wall and Chimney Shafts; and in computing such Charge the same shall be rated in Manner hereinbefore mentioned, and the Proportion such Person shall be liable to pay shall be recovered in such Manner as is hereinbefore particularly declared concerning the first Building of a Party Wall.

Section 43

London Building Act 1774

Provided always, That any Party Fence-wall, now built, or hereafter to be built, may be raised by and at the Expense of the Proprietor or Occupier of the Ground on either Side adjoining thereto; but no Party Fence-wall shall hereafter be built upon, or against, or used as a Party Wall, unless the same be of the Materials, Height, and Thickness, hereinbefore directed for Party Walls, to the Rate or Class of Building so to be erected against or upon the same: And in case of the Insufficiency of such Wall for the Purposes aforesaid, or if instead of such Party Fence-wall there be only a Wooden Fence, the Proprietor or Occupier of either of the adjoining Premises shall be at Liberty, at his own Expense, to take down such Wall or Fence, and erect a new Party Wall in lieu thereof, making good every Damage that may accrue to the adjoining Premises by such Rebuilding, so nevertheless as that such new Party Wall shall not extend on the Surface of such adjoining Ground more than Seven Inches beyond the Centre Line of such Party Fence-wall or Fence; but no Proprietor or Occupier of such adjoining Premises shall make use of such Party Wall, otherwise than as a Party Fence-wall, unless the site, or they, pay a proportionable Share of the whole Expense of erecting such Parts of such Wall, according to the Use he, she, or they, shall make of the same, at the Rates aforesaid.

Section 45
London Building Act 1774

Provided also, That in case any Such Party Wall shall extend further upon the Ground of the Party building the same than the Party Fence-wall did, yet the Party rebuilding the same shall not thereby lose any Part of the Soil whereon such Party Wall shall be built; nor shall the Owner or Owners of the other Part of Such Party Wall claim, or be entitled to, any Right of Soil, more than what he was before entitled to.